Climate and Sustainability Communication

Climate and Sustainability Communication: Global Perspectives builds upon traditional approaches to understanding the role of mass media in shaping social issues by amplifying diverse perspectives of opinion leaders, as well as voices of those affected by climate and sustainability issues.

From South Korea and China, to the United States and Zambia, the studies reported in this book—compiled using a variety of formal research methods, including content analysis, interview, and survey—emphasize cultural orientation and global implications of climate and sustainability concerns and issues. The contributors explore the cultures, geographies, and media systems underpinning climate and sustainability campaigns emerging around the world, how we theorize about them, and the ways media are used to communicate about them.

The way in which complex problems and opportunities associated with globalization and power inequities interplay with climate and sustainability communication requires creative, interdisciplinary approaches. This book opens new conversations for integrating scholarly arenas of mass media communication, science and environmental communication, political communication, and health communication, as well as their respective theory and research method sets. This book originally was published as a special issue of *Mass Communication and Society*.

Donnalyn Pompper is a Professor in the School of Media and Communication, Temple University, Philadelphia, PA, USA. Her teaching and research concerns power, the provision of routes for enabling people around the world to enjoy equality and respect at work, and critique of the ways in which social identity groups are represented across mass media platforms.

Climate and Sustainability Communication

Global Perspectives

Edited by
Donnalyn Pompper

Routledge
Taylor & Francis Group

LONDON AND NEW YORK

First published 2017 by Routledge

2 Park Square, Milton Park, Abingdon, Oxfordshire OX14 4RN
52 Vanderbilt Avenue, New York, NY 10017

Routledge is an imprint of the Taylor & Francis Group, an informa business

First issued in paperback 2018

British Library Cataloguing in Publication Data
A catalogue record for this book is available from the British Library

ISBN 13: 978-0-415-78899-1 (hbk)
ISBN 13: 978-0-367-21858-4 (pbk)

Typeset in TimesNewRomanPS
by diacriTech, Chennai

Publisher's Note
The publisher accepts responsibility for any inconsistencies that may have arisen
during the conversion of this book from journal articles to book chapters, namely
the possible inclusion of journal terminology.

Disclaimer
Every effort has been made to contact copyright holders for their permission to
reprint material in this book. The publishers would be grateful to hear from any
copyright holder who is not here acknowledged and will undertake to rectify any
errors or omissions in future editions of this book.

Contents

CONTENTS

Citation Information

The chapters in this book were originally published in *Mass Communication and Society*, volume 19, issue 5 (September–October 2016). When citing this material, please use the original page numbering for each article, as follows:

Introduction
Beyond the Business Case: Building Upon Traditional Approaches and Opening New Spaces for Multiple Perspectives on Climate and Sustainability Communication
Donnalyn Pompper
Mass Communication and Society, volume 19, issue 5 (September–October 2016) pp. 543–547

Chapter 1
Mass Communication Research in Sustainability Science: Moving Toward an Engaged Approach to Address Society's Sustainability Dilemma
Hollie Smith, Brianne Suldovsky, and Laura Lindenfeld
Mass Communication and Society, volume 19, issue 5 (September–October 2016) pp. 548–565

Chapter 2
Who Is Responsible for Climate Change? Attribution of Responsibility, News Media and South Koreans' Perceived Risk of Climate Change
Jeongheon JC Chang, Sei-Hill Kim, Jae Chul Shim, and Dong Hoon Ma
Mass Communication and Society, volume 19, issue 5 (September–October 2016) pp. 566–584

Chapter 3
Marketplace Advocacy by the U.S. Fossil Fuel Industries: Issues of Representation and Environmental Discourse
Barbara Miller Gaither and T. Kenn Gaither
Mass Communication and Society, volume 19, issue 5 (September–October 2016) pp. 585–603

CITATION INFORMATION

Chapter 4

Digital Media, Cycle of Contention, and Sustainability of Environmental Activism: The Case of Anti-PX Protests in China
Jun Liu
Mass Communication and Society, volume 19, issue 5 (September–October 2016) pp. 604–625

Chapter 5

Media's Role in Enhancing Sustainable Development in Zambia
Carrie Young and Katherine McComas
Mass Communication and Society, volume 19, issue 5 (September–October 2016) pp. 626–649

Chapter 6

"Maybe Yes, Maybe No?": Testing the Indirect Relationship of News Use through Ambivalence and Strength of Policy Position on Public Engagement with Climate Change
Jay D. Hmielowski and Erik C. Nisbet
Mass Communication and Society, volume 19, issue 5 (September–October 2016) pp. 650–670

Chapter 7

Communicating Sustainability Online: An Examination of Corporate, Nonprofit, and University Websites
Holly Ott, Ruoxu Wang, and Denise Bortree
Mass Communication and Society, volume 19, issue 5 (September–October 2016) pp. 671–687

For any permission-related enquiries please visit:
http://www.tandfonline.com/page/help/permissions

Notes on Contributors

Denise Bortree is an Associate Professor in the College of Communications, Pennsylvania State University, University Park, PA, USA. Her research interests include sustainability, nonprofit communication, and corporate social responsibility.

Jeongheon JC Chang is an Associate Professor in the Department of Health and Strategic Communication, CHA University, Pangyo, South Korea. His research interests include health and risk communication.

T. Kenn Gaither is a Professor in the School of Communications, Elon University, Elon, NC, USA. His research interests include international public relations, public relations, persuasion, and propaganda.

Jay D. Hmielowski is an Assistant Professor in the Edward R. Murrow College of Communication, Washington State University, Pullman, WA, USA. His research interests include political and environmental communication.

Sei-Hill Kim is a Professor in the School of Journalism and Mass Communications, University of South Carolina, Columbia, SC, USA. His research interests include health and science communication.

Laura Lindenfeld is a Professor in the Margaret Chase Smith Policy Center, University of Maine, Orono, ME, USA. Her research interests include science communication and sustainability science.

Jun Liu is an Assistant Professor in the Department of Media, Cognition and Communication and at the Centre for Communication and Computing, University of Copenhagen, Denmark. His research interests include political communication, information and communication technologies, and political sociology.

Dong Hoon Ma is a Professor in the School of Media and Communication, Korea University, Seoul, South Korea. His research interests include cultural studies.

Katherine McComas is a Professor in the Department of Communication, Cornell University, Ithaca, NY, USA. Her research interests include the ways to develop risk messages that encourage greater awareness of the public health implications of climate change, species conservation, and biodiversity and public acceptability of risk in the context of new and renewable energy technologies.

Barbara Miller Gaither is an Associate Professor in the School of Communications, Elon University, Elon, NC, USA. Her research interests include marketplace advocacy and corporate advocacy, crisis and risk communication, and issue advertising.

Erik C. Nisbet is an Associate Professor in the School of Communication, Ohio State University, Columbus, OH, USA. His research interests include political and environmental communication.

Holly Ott is an Assistant Professor in the School of Journalism and Mass Communications, University of South Carolina, Columbia, SC, USA. Her research interests include corporate social responsibility communication.

Donnalyn Pompper is a Professor in the School of Media and Communication, Temple University, Philadelphia, PA, USA. Her teaching and research concerns power, the provision of routes for enabling people around the world to enjoy equality and respect at work, and critique of the ways in which social identity groups are represented across mass media platforms.

Jae Chul Shim is a Professor in the School of Media and Communication, Korea University, Seoul, South Korea. His research interests include media and political communication.

Hollie Smith is an Assistant Professor in the Harrington School of Communication, University of Rhode Island, Kingston, RI, USA. Her research interests include the intersections of media, science, and policy.

Brianne Suldovsky is a Postdoctoral Fellow in the Science of Science Communication at the Annenberg Public Policy Center, University of Pennsylvania, Philadelphia, PA, USA. Her research interests include the philosophy and practice of science communication.

Ruoxu Wang is a PhD candidate in the College of Communications, Pennsylvania State University, University Park, PA, USA. Her research interests include communication technology, strategic communication, and human–computer interaction.

Carrie Young is a doctoral student in the Department of Communication, Cornell University, Ithaca, NY, USA. Her research interests include environmental, health, and risk communication with a focus on the use of media around sustainability issues in sub-Saharan Africa.

INTRODUCTION

Beyond the Business Case: Building Upon Traditional Approaches and Opening New Spaces for Multiple Perspectives on Climate and Sustainability Communication

Donnalyn Pompper
School of Media & Communication
Temple University

This *Mass Communication and Society* special issue acknowledges roles of mass media and other communication forms in a context of sustainability and global climate risk and argues for making communication a key component of sustainability science research and practice—not only as a one-way self-promotion form, but also as a facilitator of two-way communication among stakeholders for authenticity, understanding, and problem solving. Although a business case model has proven useful in convincing some organizational members to adopt sustainability measures in order to protect profits, a significant downside has been a depreciation of the social goals of protecting people and the planet. These are serious global concerns. The stakes are high. The health and well-being of humans and other living things hang in the balance (Maibach, Roser-Renouf, & Leiserowitz, 2008). When controversial or otherwise divisive science issues become shrouded in a business case argument for cost reduction (e.g., avoiding litigation costs, boycotts and other activist mobilization), organizations' responsibilities to the planet and future generations may become obscured.

This special issue was designed to propel research about climate and sustainability communication beyond our field's initial and near-exclusive

1

attention to news media—and toward greater understanding of the larger picture—to the cultures, geographies, and mind-sets underpinning climate and sustainability campaigns emerging around the world, albeit too slowly for some of us. In the call for papers for this special issue, I asked for new research that goes beyond offering up business-case approaches so common among U.S.-based research on corporate social responsibility and sustainability. The critical approaches and tone taken by our authors open new conversations for integrating arenas of mass communication, science and environmental communication, political communication, health communication, and their respective theory and research method sets—as means to interrogate issues associated with climate and sustainability communication. Combined, an interdisciplinary focus provides clear perspectives on the interconnected ways that society and mass media shape and influence climate and sustainability communication dialog and potential solutions. Dozens of manuscripts were submitted for consideration from nations including Belgium, Denmark, Germany, People's Republic of China, South Korea, and the United States. Those accepted after blind peer review address climate and sustainability communication from a broad global perspective, of course, but offer specific investigations for context with solid recommendations for moving forward. Throughout, this issue's articles represent use of both qualitative and quantitative research methods and incorporate a number of theoretical underpinnings.

First up, Hollie Smith, Brianne Suldovsky, and Laura Lindenfeld offer an essay that advocates for an integrated, transdisciplinary team approach to sustainability science for empowering researchers to employ agenda-setting and framing theories in new ways for a more engaged role in sustainability science research and practice.

Survey findings from Jeongheon JC Chang, Sei-Hill Kim, Jae Chul Shim, and Dong Hoon Ma highlight ways that South Koreans' news media use for science information may be associated with the way they attribute responsibility for climate change. In particular, findings suggest that use of online bulletin boards and blogs is positively associated with blame directed at government and corporations.

Barbara Miller Gaither and T. Kenn Gaither employed a cultural-economic model of public relations and a semiological approach to examine website advertising of U.S.-based industry trade groups representing the fossil fuel industries. Perhaps unsurprisingly, findings reveal climate discourse shaped by wealthy industry trade groups that steer public dialogue away from climate change and potential environmental policies—and toward ways that such policies might hurt the industries and adversely affect average U.S. citizens.

Next, Jun Liu presents a case study about seven anti-petrochemical protests in China from 2007 to 2014 and offers findings of 54 in-depth interviews, employing the concept of "cycles of contention" to investigate recurrent mechanisms of protest in contemporary society, with a focus on digitally mediated environmental activism.

Interviews with farmers in Zambia provided Carrie Young and Katherine McComas with a substantive data set for probing the role of media in advancing sustainable development there. Their study investigating impact of a novel program involving radio broadcasts, books, and interpersonal dialog for dealing with localized dual pressures of climate change and population growth challenges across the continent of Africa reveals findings that suggest new ways for transcending enduring infrastructure, geography, and resource challenges. These are important initiatives for reaching as many people as possible with appropriate innovations.

Jay D. Hmielowski and Erik C. Nisbet used national online survey findings to probe the role of political ideology as it moderates indirect effects of conservative and nonconservative media use through intra-attitudinal consistency (i.e., ambivalence) and strength of policy position (i.e., how strongly people support or oppose mitigation policies) on intention to take political action regarding the issue of climate change. Findings suggest that conservative media use increases intention to take political action through two intervening variables among conservatives and moderates—and decreases engagement through the same variables among liberals. Results for nonconservative media use suggest similar findings in the opposite direction.

Finally, Holly Ott, Ruoxu Wang, and Denise Bortree content analyzed sets of corporate, nonprofit, and university websites to assess online communication about sustainability. Findings suggest significant attention to sustainability among corporate and university websites, but far less attention among nonprofits' websites. The authors also address implications of quantifying sustainability claims on those websites.

Climate justice is a social justice issue. Corporate social responsibility and sustainability debates have opened new government–business–society dialogs that did not exist on a large scale 25 years ago (Pompper, 2015). Although the transformative potential of organizations and interested stakeholders to work together for positive change is significant, we're seeing a decline in cross-class civic federations and the rise in trends such as "slacktivism" or "clicktivism" (Karpf, 2010, p. 1) and armchair activism when widespread and well-managed climate movement action is necessary (Skocpol, 2013). Publicly traded companies operating within a free-market economy carefully consider business case arguments when any proposed infrastructural organizational change is considered —the kind of change required to offset negative effects of climate change. Corporations are well positioned to broaden the scope of operations beyond profit-centric goals in order to make deep change a reality. Moreover, policymakers, together with citizens, workers, and voters, must move through "elitist discourse" for global responses and actions aimed at reducing climate change threats now (Beck, 2010, p. 254). Paradoxically, it seems that merely providing the general public with scientific evidence may not be enough to change their minds or to motivate climate change action (Hennes, Ruisch, Feygina, Monteiro, & Jost, 2016), an outcome also attended to in this special issue (Hmielowski, Nisbet, & Kim). As our group of special issue authors point out, whether it's websites, radio, advertising, or news media, mass media shape our attention to, predispositions toward, perceptions of, and actions regarding problems with political implications—issues that concern all of us.

Many important questions remain for future investigation. It is my hope that these seven pieces of new research inspire new conversations, debates, and additional inquiries as we collectively tackle climate and sustainability communication. This set of articles constitutes a good start in expanding theory-building enterprises with practical implications for better understanding of climate and sustainability communication. Moving forward, I encourage greater attention to what some have argued is the crux of the climate change issue—that the disagreement stems from whether the problem exists at all rather than on how best to take corrective action (Hennes et al., 2016). I also recommend sharper focus on use of social media as a medium for persuading citizens and pressuring opinion leaders for positive climate and sustainability action. Scrutiny of online bulletin boards and blogs in South Korea (Chang, Seihill, Shim, & Ma) emphasizes urgency for even more research about nonmainstream, or noncorporate, news sources available via the Internet and social media. It is here where media may best serve as change agent in course correcting where climate change and sustainability are at issue. Even though researchers have been attracted to advocacy organizations' impact on politics in the United States, precisely how these work remains relatively unknown (Hestres, 2014). Moreover, only one of the articles in this special issue (Young & McComas) explores sustainability issues south of the equator. More research on climate and sustainability communication as it affects the Global South sorely is needed. Complex problems and opportunities associated with globalization and power inequities require interdisciplinary, creative approaches. Let's keep rolling.

REFERENCES

Beck, U. (2010). Climate for change, or how to create a green modernity. *Theory, Culture & Society, 27*, 254–266.

Hennes, E. P., Ruisch, B. C., Feygina, I., Monteiro, C. A., & Jost, J. T. (2016). Motivated recall in the service of the economic system: The case of anthropogenic climate change. *Journal of Experimental Psychology: General, 145*, 755–771.

Hestres, L. (2014). Preaching to the choir: Internet-mediated advocacy, issue public mobilization, and climate change. *New Media & Society, 16*, 323–339.

Karpf, D. (2010). Online political mobilization from the advocacy group's perspective: Looking beyond clicktivism. *Policy & Internet, 2*(4), 1–35.

Maibach, E., Roser-Renouf, C., & Leiserowitz, A. (2008). Communication and marketing as climate change intervention assets: A public health perspective. *American Journal of Preventive Medicine, 35*, 488–500.

Pompper, D. (2015). *Corporate social responsibility, sustainability, and public relations: Negotiating multiple complex challenges.* New York, NY: Routledge.

Skocpol, T. (2013, January). *Naming the problem: What it will take to counter extremism and engage Americans in the fight against global warming.* Paper presented at the symposium on The Politics of America's Fight Against Global Warming, Harvard University, Cambridge, MA. Retrieved from http://www.scholarsstrategynetwork.org/sites/default/files/skocpol_captrade_report_january_2013_0.pdf

Mass Communication Research in Sustainability Science: Moving Toward an Engaged Approach to Address Society's Sustainability Dilemma

Hollie Smith
Harrington School of Communication
University of Rhode Island

Brianne Suldovsky
Communication and Journalism
University of Maine

Laura Lindenfeld
Margaret Chase Smith Policy Center
University of Maine

Mass communication scholarship provides invaluable insight into how discursive trends in media reflect, produce, and obscure society's most pressing sustainability issues, yet too often this research falls short of creating action, interventions, or change. In this article, we argue that mass communication should be considered a cornerstone discipline for sustainability science research, particularly within transdisiciplinary sustainability science teams. We contend that mass communication researchers can advance sustainability efforts by moving toward a more engaged approach. In an effort to support scholars' transition to such engagement, we consider how traditional mass communication theories can add value to action-oriented transdisciplinary sustainability science efforts and provide examples of engaged, transdisciplinary mass communication scholarship.

INTRODUCTION

The special call for this issue of *Mass Communication and Society* raised a key question: What are the roles of mass media and other forms of communication with regard to climate and sustainability programs? This question is particularly relevant given the rapid advancement in global risks we face as a society. As we consider communication's role within climate and sustainability programs, we extend this line of questioning to reevaluate the role of mass media and communication researchers within sustainability research and practice as well. Mass media and communication scholars have long studied sustainability issues (e.g., Lewis, 2000; Nielsen & Kjærgaard, 2011; Su, Akin, Brossard, Scheufele, & Xenos, 2015) from a wide range of methodological and theoretical traditions. Scholars have produced expansive quantitative studies on the trends in media coverage of climate change (e.g., Uzelgun & Castro, 2015), sustainable food systems (Lockie, 2006), and sustainability at large (Barkemeyer, Figge, Holt, & Wettstein, 2009), whereas others have taken a critical perspective and focused qualitative critiques on gendered and racial stereotypes portrayed in popular films about climate change and sustainability (e.g., McGreavy & Lindenfeld, 2014). Although this diverse body of mass communication scholarship has advanced disciplinary understanding of media trends and effects, it often times fails to engage questions about what, if anything, should be done to change these discursive productions. Mass communication research is inherently a socially relevant line of research, and we see key areas of growth for the field in integrating mass communication scholarship with research being done in trans-disciplinary sustainability science teams that are focused on solving pressing societal problems.

Sustainability science has developed in an attempt to address society's most complex environmental, economic, and social problems, and it calls for a new level of engagement from academics and citizens alike. Sustainability science posits that transdisciplinary teams of scholars, decision makers, and stakeholders from various backgrounds can produce more actionable results than any of these groups individually (van Kerkhoff & Lebel, 2006); we see mass communication research as a key part of this effort. Mass communication scholarship is so vastly important to include in sustainability science work as it helps us understand human and social behavior in response to sustainability crises. Media effects theories in particular offer a crucial understanding of how discourses circulate, how dominant narratives emerge, and how those discourses and narratives relate to perceptions, intentions, and action.

In this article, we argue for the inclusion of mass communication scholarship, and media effects research in particular, in transdisciplinary sustainability science efforts. We provide an overview of sustainability science as an action-oriented field of inquiry and review mass communication researchers limited role in the field to date. We then identify key theoretical constructs in mass communication scholarship that offer potential paths forward for mass media scholars who are attempting to adopt an engaged approach. Finally, we conclude with an overview of the types of work mass communication scholars can contribute to sustainability research and practice. The implications of this type of integration are discussed.

SUSTAINABILITY SCIENCE

The 21st century has seen the emergence of global risks that threaten the sustainability of earth's resources like no other time in history, including declines in eco-diversity (Thuiller, Lavorel, Araujo, Sykes, & Prentice, 2005), increasing ocean acidification (Johnson & White, 2014) and climate change (Costello et al., 2009). As a result of these rapidly changing global conditions, scientists, decision makers, and governmental organizations have advanced new ways to study, understand, and address problems in such diverse contexts (Beck, 1992). Through these advancements, sustainability science emerged as an action-oriented line of research aimed at addressing complex sustainability problems that span different regions, cultures, and scales (Brown, Harris, & Russell, 2010; Kates et al., 2001; Kreuter, Rosa, Howze, & Baldwin, 2004). These constantly fluctuating issues represent "wicked problems," in that they cannot be solved with simple singular solutions. Wicked problems, like climate change, are difficult to define and operationalize because of their multifaceted nature and the changing context in which they exist. Using climate change as an example, there are human, economic, and ecosystem dimensions to this particularly "wicked" problem, and the complexity surfaces through an intricate tapestry of other issues: increased drought, food scarcity, more exaggerated weather patterns and extreme storms, natural resource management, and national and global policy, to name a few. Addressing wicked problems with a sustainability science approach requires researchers to move beyond disciplinary expertise and adopt a more holistic systems perspective. Sustainability science is distinct in its theoretical premise that social-ecological systems (SES) are interdependent and cannot be separated in study or practice. To fully understand how SES processes are interconnected, the SES approach requires the work of transdisciplinary researchers, practitioners, and stakeholders. This type of team-based approach aims to not only integrate different social and ecological understandings into sustainability but also result in more feasible solutions for the given social and cultural context (W. C. Clark et al., 2011).

At the heart of sustainability science lies the assumption that knowledge can and will be moved into the realm of action and decision making (W. C. Clark et al., 2011). This fundamental assumption of sustainability science necessitates including stakeholders and communities in research to increase its likelihood of being used in decision making (W. C. Clark et al., 2011). Based on the notion that there are no panaceas (Ostrom, Janssen, & Anderies, 2007), we see examples of this stakeholder-inclusive approach in literatures such as Mode 2 science (Gibbons et al., 1994), community engagement (Weerts & Sandmann, 2010), boundary work (Guston, 2001; Weerts & Sandmann, 2010), knowledge coproduction (Cornwell & Campbell, 2012), and collaborative resilience (Goldstein, 2011). Despite the adoption of new stakeholder-inclusive approaches to sustainability science, it remains a complex and challenging process (e.g. Corner, Pidgeon, & Parkhill, 2012; Pomeranz et al., 2014; Ramachandra & Naha Abu Mansor, 2014).

Although some critical communication scholars have moved toward stakeholder-inclusive methods that parallel the sustainability science approach, mass communication scholars have been slower to integrate this engagement into scholarship. This lack of engagement is not unique to mass communication research, as traditional scientific approaches have a large degree of separation between knowledge producers and users, and often assume that knowledge will "trickle down and transfer" to society (van Kerkhoff & Lebel, 2006). And although this is certainly the dominant approach in mass communication research and science more broadly, this model has frequently resulted in a fundamental disconnection between researchers who play an important role in knowledge production and people who may use the knowledge in practice (van Kerkhoff & Lebel, 2006 p. 449). In response to this disconnection, sustainability science uses transdisciplinarity as one mechanism to generate more capacity for linking knowledge and action (Cash, Borck, & Patt, 2006; Lemos & Morehouse, 2005; Pohl, 2008). Transdisciplinarity requires an iterative approach to research, where researchers work beyond disciplinary boundaries to engage stakeholders in the creation and implementation of research-based policies and projects. Key here is the need for the mutual understanding that diverse kinds of knowledge have value and must be included in research design, data collection, and knowledge outcomes. Within transdisciplinary sustainability science, researchers have one type of knowledge and stakeholders have another, and both have equal valuation in the research process (Anadón, Giménez, Ballestar, & Pérez, 2009; Hage, Leroy, & Petersen, 2010).

Communication research on a broader scale has made some inroads into these sustainability science efforts (Lindenfeld, Hall, McGreavy, Silka, & Hart, 2012), whereas mass communication research has yet to become an integral part of any transdisciplinary efforts (Smith & Lindenfeld, 2014). This lack of integration may partly be caused by the hands-off nature and methodology of most mass communication research. Looking at traditional mass communication studies, we see that scholars track trends in media (Uzelgun & Castro, 2015), correlate media agendas to public agendas (McCombs & Reynolds, 2009), examine the effects of framing and content (Cobb, 2005; Donk, Metag, Kohrin, & Marcinkowksi, 2012; Tewksbury & Scheufele, 2009), and critique stereotypical portrayals of marginalized groups (McGreavy & Lindenfeld, 2015). These studies are essential to understanding media processes, trends, and effects, yet they rely on quantitative and qualitative analysis of count, survey, or thematic data, and rarely, if ever, require engagement with scientists from other disciplines or the direct engagement with human subjects. Even more distinct is the lack of stakeholder inclusion in mass communication research, be it the inclusion of local media consumers, journalists, or diverse voices.

Mass communication researchers need to be included in these transdisciplinary efforts, as media effects theories offer a crucial understanding of issues that these teams deal with in almost every issue: why people perceive sustainability issues in certain ways and what shapes their behavior in response. If mass communication theories are ignored in the sustainability science design, we risk missing an understanding of how mass media play a key role in creating a shared cultural understanding of sustainability phenomena in our communities, nationally, and globally. Inclusion in this important effort, however, does not just mean answering a transdisciplinary research call. Mass communication researchers can enter an important new area by more aptly taking into account a diverse group of stakeholders and researchers in our research questions, design, and methodological choices. Even more, this move would rearticulate communication processes and expand them beyond the traditional transmission model, including mass communication scholars in the move "from deficit to dialogue" (Bucchi, 2008) that is evident in other communication fields. We certainly do not argue that all mass communication research should be directly engaged in transdisciplinary efforts with stakeholders. Rather, we see this as one important pathway forward for mass communication research that is too important to ignore. Mass communication researchers have crucial insights to offer this important scientific endeavor to solve problems, and this transdisciplinary move within sustainability science offers a key opportunity to grow in our own methodological approaches and theoretical assumptions.

MASS MEDIA STUDIES' INTEGRATION INTO SUSTAINABILITY SCIENCE

Given the sustainability science approach, the fundamental question we seek to answer here is how mass communication researchers in particular can play a contributing role within this expanding line of work. García-Jiménez & Craig (2010) posed the question more broadly to communication scholars at large:

> Behind the question of whether communication research has made a difference in communication practices or outcomes lies a deeper question about the specific quality of our discipline's contribution to society, however large or small that contribution may have been to date: *What kind of difference do we want to make?* (p. 429)

These types of social and ethical questions are brought to the forefront of research when dealing with sustainability issues that fundamentally impact societies' understanding of global and local risks, along with what options are feasible for mitigating them.

Mass communication scholarship offers key understandings like no other discipline into how messages are created and circulated throughout society; mass media scholars have distinct contributions to make in the emerging field of sustainability science for this very reason. The rapid expanse and global reach of social media and online news platforms further justify the inclusion of media effects scholars in transdisciplinary sustainability science efforts. We see the opportunity to include multiple mass communication theories into the sustainability science framework, but in an effort to start the conversation, we focus solely on framing and agenda-setting in this article. The knowledge that these two theories bring to bear on sustainability science issues is too large to ignore. Framing and agenda setting offer key understanding of how people come to understand and respond to changing social, environmental, and economic circumstances (Kahneman, 2011). If sustainability science is truly interested in understanding both the social and ecological dimensions of society's most pressing problems, we must fully engage media's role(s) in defining the nature of both the problems and solutions. In an effort to support this move, we explore the integration of framing and agenda-setting into the sustainability context.

Framing

The concept of framing has been used in research studies that envelop a myriad of disciplines, including communication (D'Angelo, 2006; Tuchman, 1978), sociology (Goffman, 1974), and public policy (Entman, 2004). Framing researchers within the media effects tradition work to understand the relationship between media frames, perceptions, attitudes, and beliefs while attempting to understand why certain frames are more effective at influencing audiences than others.

Journalists construct news frames that reflect cultural themes and narratives within a society and influence *how* newsreaders understand contemporary events (Price, Tewksbury, & Powers, 1997). Studies have shown that news frames can produce an observable framing effect upon readers who attended to the news (Johnson-Cartee, 2005, p. 26). Within sustainability contexts, framing offers an avenue for understanding why audiences might view sustainability problems in a certain way. What's more, framing theory offers insight into how narratives about feasible solutions are created, circulated, and validated or discarded. As mass communication scholars, taking our media research into an action-oriented transdisciplinary context we could find a new opportunity to reorient our research questions: Instead of just asking whose voices are being included in the framing of these issues, we could more fundamentally ask how to actively participate in changing the frame to be more inclusive of diverse voices and types of knowledge. Indeed, Carragee and Roefs (2004) argued that there has been a general neglect in framing research when it comes to broader implications of media power in relation to social conditions and political hegemony. The authors call for a reintegration of these considerations into framing research, making it more than just a reduction to media effects.

When we view a frame in a news text as an imprint of power (Deetz, 1992; Derrida, 2006; Entman, 2007), we can fully view how power impacts perceptions of the public on social issues (D'Angelo & Lombard, 2008; Hansen, 2000). One clear example of where this power is evident is the use of elite sources in media coverage of sustainability issues such as climate change. Research has shown how journalists aim to provide fair balance by using routine sourcing practices that would garner multiple sides to a story (Dunwoody & Ryan, 1983; Fishman, 1980; Gandy, 1982). This particular professional norm often leads to the framing of issues in a dichotomous format, with sources being categorized as for or against an issue (Leibler & Bendix, 1996; Mazur, 1990; Sigal, 1973; Smith, 1993; Smith & Norton, 2013). The media usually rely on elite government sources for technical information (Smith & Norton, 2013; Toumey, 1996) and activists or laypeople for the human dimension to the story (Greenberg, Sachsman, Sandman, & Salomone, 1989; Sandman, Weinstein, & Klotz, 1987; West, Sandman, & Greenberg, 1995). The effects of this documented practice should not be understated (Brown, Bybee, Wearden, & Straughan, 1987); Examples of how these sourcing practices impact audiences' understanding and response to social and environmental risks have been documented in cases of radon

(Cole, 1993; Sandman, Weinstein, & Klotz, 1987), arsenic (Smith et al, 2014; Susarla, 2003), and climate change (Boykoff & Boykoff, 2007). Indeed, the proliferation of the "balance as bias" (Boykoff & Boykoff, 2007) frame, where climate change deniers are given equal space in media coverage as climate change scientists, is one critical factor in the continued debate of climate change's existence even when there is an undoubted degree of certainty within the scientific community that climate change is real. Oreskes (2004) noted these effects: "Policy-makers and the media, particularly in the United States, frequently assert that climate science is highly uncertain. Some have used this as an argument against adopting strong measures to reduce greenhouse gas emissions" (p. 1686). This is particularly troubling within the sustainability science context, as audiences' ability to act on society's biggest risks is fundamentally linked to their understanding of that issue and its consequences.

Studies of source use indicate that journalists rely on elite sources when covering almost every type of news story, but particularly those focusing on issues with an environmental component (Lacy & Coulson, 2000), yet interventions to change these sourcing practices are not prevalent in the literature. The lack of research on how to modify and expand routine sourcing practices is important because it brings to light important questions of whose story is not being told, whose voices are not being heard, and who is benefitting from a narrative of uncertainty and "balance." The exclusion of some groups from these sustainability frames is troubling, as it leaves the definitions of problem and solution in the hands of an elite few.

We view an engaged approach as a unique opportunity to start a conversation on how to more actively participate in the processes that create these journalistic norms and routines, and thus the resulting frames. One proposed way to engage this issue more fully is workshops that include journalists, scientists, and policymakers (Smith & Lindenfeld, 2014). Taking our work as media scholars into the engaged realm fundamentally moves us from just tracking framing trends to more deeply participating in the active creation of future frames about sustainability problems and solutions.

One example of a transdisciplinary workshop aimed at these goals is the Metcalf Institute for Marine and Environmental Reporting at the University of Rhode Island (metcalfinstitute.org). The Metcalf Institute conducts workshops each year that bring together journalists, scientists, and stakeholders to discuss how to write about scientific studies with more cultural, scientific, and political knowledge, with key attention being paid to different scientific and stakeholder perspectives. Efforts like those of Metcalf are an important step in the right direction, and mass communication scholars can play an important role in supporting and participating in such events. Transdisciplinary workshops, projects, and research efforts can serve as an important avenue for media scholars to actively participate in moving knowledge of media systems and effects into an arena for creating solutions. Although framing provides an avenue through which mass communication scholars can understand and engage multiple voices within sustainability science contexts, it does not provide a method of understanding the role of mass media within political systems of decision making. In an effort to better understand this role, we turn to agenda-setting literature.

Agenda-Setting

Agenda-setting offers an important understanding of system dynamics and mass media influence. Agenda-setting has been one of the most frequently cited theories within published mass communication research in late 20th century (Bryant & Miron, 2004) and offers a unique understanding of the media's role in the democratic political process. The rapid expanse of online platforms for creating and sharing news further has expanded agenda-setting studies, as audiences now have an increased ability to watch news content at different times and in different places (Dayan & Katz, 1992; Perloff, 2015). Given the reach of traditional and new media platforms, bringing agenda-setting research into transdisciplinary sustainability science teams is especially important.

Agenda-setting research allows sustainability scholars to understand how issue selection and prominence in the news influences social perceptions of what is important to society (McCombs & Reynolds, 2009). The agenda-setting process has particular relevance to sustainability science, as most global sustainability issues are *unobtrusive* to media audiences and are experienced only through the lens of the media. Issues such as climate change, ocean acidification, and loss in biodiversity are all abstract conceptions and can be hard to "experience" firsthand. Research shows that agenda-setting effects are particularly strong for unobtrusive issues (Blood, 1981; Weaver, Graber, McCombs, & Eyal, 1981; Zucker, 1978). McCombs and Reynolds (2009) explained how these effects are in response to society's need for orientation (Tolman, 1932, 1948), which allows for people to understand the relevance and uncertainty around an issue.

It's important to note that agenda-setting encompasses a two-step flow theory (e.g., Brosius & Weimann, 1996), which highlights the role of opinion leaders and interpersonal networks in media effects and emphasizes the active role audiences can play in the flow of information. Sustainability offers a unique context to critique and expand the two-step flow theory embedded within the agenda-setting framework, particularly because the role of opinion leaders in complex sustainability-related contexts is not well researched or understood (Keys, Thomsen, & Smith, 2010). First, there are often more than two steps in the flow of media communication surrounding sustainability-related issues that encourage information consumers to process information in novel ways, particularly through media channels like social media (Yeo, 2014) and mobile technology (Onnela et al., 2007). These additional steps offer a new context to study and theorize the flow of information that move beyond the two-step flow model. Second, the majority of work on agenda-setting and the two-step flow theory examines information flow surrounding issues that are "settled" or solutions that are already prescribed. Issues of sustainability do not have prescribed solutions or innovations that can be diffused easily by mass media or opinion leaders (Keys et al., 2010), making the two-step flow theory a necessary, but likely not sufficient, conceptual framework to utilize in these contexts.

In addition to critiquing and expanding the two-step flow theory, agenda-setting also provides an understanding of how media might be influencing policy. Trumbo (1995) examined the influences of the media agenda on both public and political agendas in regard to global warming and found that agenda-setting effects were stronger in members of Congress than the general public. Although media scholars have documented agenda-setting effects of media coverage on policy agendas (Soroka, 2002), the argument for a two-way flow of interaction between media and policy is starting to emerge (Kiss, 2013; Tresch, Sciarini, & Varone, 2013). Even given the uncertain nature of the relationship between the press and policy, agenda-setting literature should be considered in sustainability science research aimed at changing political decision making about wicked problems.

If mass media researchers were to bring agenda-setting research into the sustainability science context, it would highlight a much messier web of influence beyond a one- or two-way flow of information. It would expand agenda-setting research questions into not just ones of media and policy, but media and policy as being interacting agents within environmental, cultural, and economic systems, where power and privilege play an important role in system dynamics. Understanding agenda-setting processes within a social ecological systems framework move us from thinking linearly about media to policy or vice versa, and moves us to a constitutive model with multiple levels of influence from inside and outside of the system. Research questions would focus not only on how the process of agenda-setting happens but also on what ecological, economic, and cultural consequences it brings.

Geographer Jared Diamond (2006) highlighted the importance of considering our work within a specific cultural and social context. His book *Collapse: How Societies Choose to Fail or Succeed* offers an important understanding of why some cultures are able to adapt to extreme environmental circumstances and some are not. This systems view of communication, culture, and the environment lends to our understanding that agenda-setting effects may be more pronounced or disappear, depending on the context. It highlights the importance of variables of culture and social identity and supports the need to take a systems view in mass communication research. We understand culture as the lived experiences of people that manifest themselves in daily rituals and practices. Cultural practices emerge within particular societies at particular times and culture functions as a domain that is dynamic, evolving, and deeply interconnected within social-ecological systems. Sustainability problems can be adequately addressed only when solutions integrate with cultural frameworks. This means, especially in heterogeneous societies like the United States, attending to diverse, often conflicting beliefs, attitudes, values, and perceptions. Benhabib (2002) emphasized that society "presents itself through narratively contested accounts" and cultures themselves emerge through "contested practices" (p. viii). For sustainability science to achieve its goals, assessment of belief and perceptions held and maintained by different segments of the population needs to be granted greater priority, especially in the context of agenda-setting, where cultural forces influence how information flows and how decision-making processes work. Social identity politics shape how change can—or cannot—happen. This, however, requires careful attention to issues of culture, the same kinds of issues that drive agenda-setting and that deserve thorough examination and consideration. As Munshi and Kurian (2005) write, "Such an acknowledgement would need to break down the hierarchy of publics and take into account the resistance of marginalized publics."

Agenda-setting clearly does not exist in a vacuum. Integrating agenda-setting theories to wicked problems and providing adequate insight into cultural contexts could not offer an understanding of how media and political agendas influence one another but could allow media scholars to more externally validate other variables that might be at play in these processes. If media scholars move beyond quantitative studies of agenda-setting effects and start working within transdisciplinary efforts, we can more realistically understand disconnects in discourse at different points within a system (where those points can be understood as science, media, policy, or others). Although this type of work with solution-oriented goals seems difficult and unlikely, sustainability scientists are calling on these collaborative processes to be integration sites in a way we have not seen before (Brown et al., 2010). In the following section, we explore how mass communication research can embrace and contribute to sustainability science within transdisciplinary contexts.

MASS COMMUNICATION RESEARCHERS IN THE
TRANSDISCIPLINARY CONTEXT

There are a multitude of avenues through which mass communication scholars can enter the world of sustainability-oriented research. In the previous section, we explored how two mass communication theories, framing and agenda-setting, could fit into sustainability settings. In this final section, we explore how this shift in the role(s) of mass communication research in sustainability contexts creates a notable change in the ethical implications of mass communication scholarship. To do this, we outline two key ethical implications and suggest avenues for mass communication scholars to grapple with these complexities.

First and foremost, the inclusion of media studies into transdisciplinary sustainability science necessitates that mass communication scholars rearticulate the overall goal of their work. Specifically, sustainability contexts demand that mass communication scholars move from describing mass media contexts to being dedicated to improving those contexts. What's more, mass communication scholars will more fully engage with how their work is or is not used in creating system dynamics that create change in social, economic, or environmental circumstances. That is, within sustainability science, documenting and describing mass communication trends, like the prevalence of frames or sourcing practices, is only the beginning step in our research design. Mass communication scholars in the transdisciplinary context must go one step further, utilizing what they learn to foster action. This is an important and dramatic shift from the traditional view of academic research as being value-neutral and should not be taken lightly. It fundamentally moves scholars away from the loading dock model of scientific knowledge production (van Kerkhoff & Lebel, 2006) into an area where knowledge coproduction is integrated into discussion, decision making, and action. As Deetz (2008) noted, "This is not a question of what *they* do with *our* knowledge, but what we and they become in producing this rather than that knowledge" (p. 291). This line of inquiry changes everything from our research questions to methodological choices, yet offers a new area for learning in a complex and vibrant real-world laboratory where media frames and agendas interact with economic, environmental, and cultural variables. Working with scholars from fields like economics, public policy, and natural science helps us better understand these variables and their role in media effects. What's more, working with stakeholders and policymakers make us more inclined to ask solutions-oriented questions with the applicability of results in mind.

Second, and related to the goal of contextual improvement, the inclusion of mass communication in sustainability science necessitates that mass communication scholars exhibit a high degree of self-evaluation, cultural sensitivity, and adaptability (Reich & Reich, 2006) to participate in this collaborative effort. Traditional research training does not prepare scientists to communicate outside their disciplines, and this can be a difficult and time-consuming endeavor. Moving from a single disciplinary research paradigm to a transdisciplinary team can cause researchers to experience a new form of role-strain, where they face competing demands from all the different groups with which they interact (Box & Cotgrove, 1966; Parker & Crona, 2012). Yet addressing any type of wicked sustainability problem will rely on input from both social and biophysical researchers, working in tandem with diverse stakeholders. Media are an important element within this work.

In light of these complexities, mass communication scholars can follow the work of Cox (2007) and other environmental communication scholars to generate a list of the normative assumptions they make when they enter into this kind of work and then use that as a starting point for collaboration and understanding with other scholars and stakeholders. With collaboration and a willingness to move through the complexity of this type of work, mass communication scholars can become a seamless and important thread in sustainability science's efforts to address society's biggest crises.

CONCLUSION

Through this article we have argued for an expansion of mass communica-tion research into the transdisciplinary context. Given society's struggle with rapidly changing environmental, social, and economic crises, we find poign-ancy in reflecting on the role that mass communication researchers can play in understanding and improving these situations. As a field, mass commu-nication research has adopted a more hands-off approach to studying the media's role in sustainability contexts. We consider it a critical moment to reflect on scholars' ethical imperative to not only study but also participate in the production of mass media trends and effects. As Cox (2007) so elegantly noted, other fields such as conservation biology and cancer biology have adopted an action-orientation where scholars work to create recommendations with a purpose, to conserve the biosphere or eradicate cancer, without theoretical or empirical guarantees. We look to these fields for an understanding of how to unpack and articulate the implicit values and attitudes we embody when we participate in engaged and action-oriented research endeavors. Although this reflection and articulation might be messy and often times uncomfortable, we think it is important to at least consider the potential for mass communication scholars' to create collaboration and change.

The inclusion of mass communication scholarship into transdisciplinary sustainability contexts will allow for mutual growth and understanding of how social, environmental, and economic systems are intertwined. Perhaps collaborating with scholars from other fields and real-world stakeholders can provide us with a more nuanced understand of the media's role in new media environments, social decision-making contexts, and risk management behaviors. It can also open up new avenues for participatory-based research methods, which lend to real-world understanding of if and how changing media routines can impact actual behavior. This transdisciplinary context provides an opportunity to conduct our research in a multifaceted global laboratory that can aid help us move to more robust understandings of media effects in social and natural systems.

We understand that this call for engagement will be a radical departure for some scholars, and we recognize the inherent ethical complexity present in the approach we are proposing. Although we do not believe that all media scholars need to engage in this type of transdisciplinary scholarship, we see it as an important and necessary avenue forward for scholars within the field. Granted, many questions remain about what results this engaged effort could bring. However, we think it is an exciting and important time to join the conversation and effort. It is our hope that this article serves as an opening discussion of how to making media scholarship a more transdisciplinary, engaged, and action-oriented endeavor.

REFERENCES

Anadón, J. D., Giménez, A., Ballestar, R., & Pérez, I. (2009). Evaluation of local ecological knowledge as a method for collecting extensive data on animal abundance. *Conservation Biology, 23,* 617–625.

Barkemeyer, R., Figge, F., Holt, D., & Wettstein, B. (2009). What the papers say: Trends in sustainability. A comparative analysis of 115 leading national newspapers worldwide. *Journal of Corporate Citizenship, 2009*(33), 68–86.

Beck, P. U. (1992). *Risk society: Towards a new modernity.* Thousand Oaks, CA: Sage.

Bell, K., Smith, H., Butts, K., Smith, A., & Lincoln, R. (2013). Pressing the issue: Effects of news media on private well water testing behavior in Maine. *National Conference on Health Communication, Marketing, & Media,* Atlanta, Georgia.

Benhabib, S. (2002). *The claims of culture: Equality and diversity in the global era.* Princeton: NJ: Princeton University Press.

Blood, D. (1981). *Unobtrusive issues in the age-setting role of the press* (Unpublished doctoral dissertation). Syracuse University, Syracuse, NY.

Box, S., & Cotgrove, S. (1966). Scientific identity, occupational selection, and role strain. *The British Journal of Sociology, 17,* 20–28.

Boykoff, M. T., & Boykoff, J. M. (2007). Climate change and journalistic norms: A case-study of US mass-media coverage. *Geoforum, 38,* 1190–1204.

Brosius, H., & Weimann, G. (1996). Who sets the agenda: Agenda-setting as a two-step flow. *Communication Research, 23*(5), 561–580.

Brown, J. D., Bybee, C. R., Wearden, S. T., & Straughan, D. M. (1987). Invisible power: Newspaper news sources and the limits of diversity. *Journalism & Mass Communication Quarterly, 64*(1), 45–54.

CLIMATE AND SUSTAINABILITY COMMUNICATION

Brown, V. A., Harris, J. A., & Russell, J. (2010). *Tackling wicked problems through the transdisciplinary imagination*. London, UK: Earthscan.

Bryant, J., & Miron, D. (2004). Theory and research in mass communication. *Journal of Communication, 54*, 662–704.

Bucchi, M. (2008). Of deficits, deviations and dialogues: Theories of public communication of science. In M. Bucchi & B. Trench (Eds.), *Handbook of public communication of science and technology* (pp. 57–76). Florence, KY: Routledge.

Carragee, K. M., & Roefs, W. (2004). The neglect of power in recent framing research. *Journal of Communication, 54*(2), 214–233.

Cash, D. W., Borck, J. C., & Patt, A. G. (2006). Countering the loading-dock approach to linking science and decision-making: Comparative analysis of El Nino Southern Oscillation (ENSO) forecasting systems. *Science, Technology & Human Values, 31*(4), 465–494.

Clark, W. C., Tomich, T. P., van Noordwijk, M., Guston, D., Catacutan, D., & Dickson, N. M., & McNie, E. (2011). Boundary work for sustainable development: Natural resource management at the Consultative Group on International Agricultural Research (CGIAR). *Proceedings of the National Academy of Sciences*, vol. 10.1073/pnas.0900231108 .

Cobb, M. D. (2005). Framing effects on public opinion about nanotechnology. *Science Communication, 27*(2), 221–239.

Cole, L. A. (1993). *Element of risk, the politics of radon*. New York, NY: Oxford University Press.

Corner, A., Pidgeon, N., & Parkhill, K. (2012). Perceptions of geoengineering: Public attitudes, stakeholder perspectives, and the challenge of "upstream" engagement. *Wiley Interdisciplinary Reviews: Climate Change, 3*(5), 451–466. doi:10.1002/wcc.176

Cornwell, M. L., & Campbell, L. M. (2012). Co-producing conservation and knowledge: Citizen-based sea turtle monitoring in North Carolina, USA. *Social Studies of Science, 42*(1), 101–120.

Costello, A., Abbas, M., Allen, A., Ball, S., Bell, S., Bellamy, R., & Patterson, C. (2009). Managing the health effects of climate change: Lancet and University College London Institute for Global Health Commission. *The Lancet, 373*(9676), 1693–1733. doi:10.1016/S0140-6736(09)60935-1

Cox, R. (2007). Nature's "crisis disciplines": Does environmental communication have an ethical duty? *Environmental Communication, 1*(1), 5–20. doi:10.1080/17524030701333948

D'Angelo, P. (2006). News framing as a multiparidigmatic research program: A response to Entman. *Journal of Communication, 52*(4), 870–888.

D'Angelo, P., & Lombard, M. (2008). The power of the press: The effects of press frames in political campaign news on media perceptions. *Atlantic Journal of Communication, 16*, 1–32.

Dayan, D., & Katz, E. (1992). *Media events: The live broadcasting of history*. Cambridge, MA: Harvard University Press.

Deetz, S. (1992). *Democracy in an age of corporate colonization: Developments in communication and the politics of everyday life*. Albany: State University of New York Press.

Deetz, S. (2008). Engagement as co-generative theorizing. *Journal of Applied Communication Research, 36*(3), 289–297.

Derrida, J. (2006). Specters of Marx. (1st ed). New York, NY: Routledge.

Diamond, J. (2006). *Collapse: How societies choose to fail or succeed*. New York, NY: Penguin.

Donk, A., Metag, J., Kohrin, M., & Marcinkowksi, F. (2012). Framing emerging technologies: Risk perceptions of nanotechnology in the German press. *Science Communication, 34*(1), 5–29.

Dunwoody, S., & Ryan, M. (1983). Public information persons as mediators between scientists and journalists. *Journalism & Mass Communication Quarterly, 60*(4), 647–656.

Entman, R. (2004). *Projections of power: Framing news, public opinion, and U.S. foreign policy*. Chicago, IL: University of Chicago Press.

Entman, R. (2007). Framing bias: Media in the distribution of power. *Journal of Communication, 57*, 163–173.

Fishman, M. (1980). *Manufacturing the news*. Austin: University of Texas Press.

Gandy, O. (1982). *Beyond agenda setting: Information subsidies and public policy.* Norwood, NJ: Ablex.

García-Jiménez, L., & Craig, R. T. (2010). What kind of difference do we want to make? *Communication Monographs, 77*(4), 429–431. doi:10.1080/03637751.2010.523591

Gibbons, M., Limoges, C., Nowotny, H., Schwartzman, S., Scott, P., & Trow, M. (1994). *The new production of knowledge: The dynamics of science and research in contemporary societies.* London, UK: Sage.

Goffman, E. (1974). *Frame analysis: An essay on the organization of experience.* Boston, MA: Northeastern University Press.

Goldstein, B. E. (Ed.). (2011). *Collaborative resilience: Moving through crisis to opportunity.* Cambridge, MA: MIT Press.

Greenberg, M. R., Sachsman, D. B., Sandman, P. M., & Salomone, K. L. (1989). Risk, drama and geography in coverage of Environmental risk by network TV. *Journalism & Mass Communication Quarterly, 66*(2), 267–276.

Guston, D. H. (2001). Boundary organizations in environmental policy and science: An introduction. *Science, Technology, & Human Values, 26*(4), 399–408.

Hage, M., Leroy, P., & Petersen, A. C. (2010). Stakeholder participation in environmental knowledge production. *Futures, 42*(3), 254–264.

Johnson, A., & White, N. D. (2014). Ocean acidification: The other climate change issue. *American Scientist, 102*(1), 60–63.

Johnson-Cartee, K. (2005). *News narratives and news framing.* Lanham, MD: Rowman and Littlefield.

Kahneman, D. (2011). *Thinking, fast and slow.* New York, NY: Farrar, Straus and Giroux.

Kates, R. W., Clark, W. C., Corell, R., Hall, J. M., Jaeger, C. C., Lowe, I., & Svedin, U. (2001). Sustainability science. *Science, 292*, 641–642. doi:10.1126/science.1059386

Keys, N., Thomsen, D., & Smith, T. (2010). Opinion leaders and complex sustainability issues. *Management of Environmental Quality: An International Journal, 21*(2), 187–197.

Kiss, S. J. (2013). Legislation by agenda-setting: Assessing the media's role in the regulation of Bisphenol A in the U.S. States. *Mass Communication and Society, 16*(5), 687–712. doi:10.1080/15205436.2013.768345

Kreuter, M. W., Rosa, C. D., Howze, E. H., & Baldwin, G. T. (2004). Understanding wicked problems: A key to advancing environmental health promotion. *Health Education & Behavior: The Official Publication of the Society for Public Health Education, 31*, 441–454. doi:10.1177/1090198104265597

Lacy, S., & Coulson, D. (2000, Winter). Comparative case study: Newspaper source use on the environmental beat. *Newspaper Research Journal*, pp. 13–25.

Leibler, C., & Bendix, J. (1996). Old-growth forests on network news: News Sources and the framing of an environmental controversy. *Journalism & Mass Communication Quarterly, 73*(1), 53–65.

Lemos, M. C., & Morehouse, B. J. (2005). The co-production of science and policy in integrated climate assessments. *Global Environmental Change, 15*, 57–68.

Lewis, T. L. (2000). Media representations of "sustainable development": Sustaining the status quo? *Science Communication, 21*(3), 244–273. doi:10.1177/1075547000021003003

Lindenfeld, L., Hall, D., McGreavy, B., Silka, L., & Hart, D. (2012). Creating a place for environmental communication research in sustainability science. *Environmental Communication, 6*(1), 23–43. doi:10.1080/17524032.2011.640702

Lockie, S. (2006). Capturing the sustainability agenda: Organic foods and media discourses on food scares, environment, genetic engineering, and health. *Agriculture and Human Values, 23*, 313–323.

Mazur, A. (1990). Nuclear power, chemical hazards, and the quantity of reporting. *Minerva, 28*, 294–323.

McCombs, M., & Reynolds, A. (2009). How the news shapes our civic agenda. In J. Bryant & M. B. Oliver (Eds.), *Media effects: Advances in theory and research* (pp. 1–18). New York, NY: Routledge.

McGreavy, B., & Lindenfeld, L. (2014). Entertaining our way to engagement? Climate change films and sustainable development values. *International Journal of Sustainable Development, 17*(2), 123–136.

Munshi, D., & Kurian, P. (2005). Imperializing spin cycles: A postcolonial look at public relations, greenwashing, and the separation of publics. *Public Relations Review, 31*, 513–520.

Nielsen, K. H., & Kjærgaard, R. S. (2011). News coverage of climate change in nature news and science now during 2007. *Environmental Communication: A Journal of Nature and Culture, 5*(1), 25–44. doi:10.1080/17524032.2010.520722

Onnela, J., Saramaki, J., Hyvonen, J., Szabo, G., Lazer, D., Kaski, K., … Barabasi, A. (2007). Structure and tie strengths in mobile communication networks. *Proceedings of the National Academy of Sciences of the United States of America, 104*(18), 7332–7336.

Oreskes, N. (2004). The scientific consensus on climate change. *Science, 306*(5702), 1686.

Ostrom, E., Janssen, M. A., & Anderies, J. M. (2007). Going beyond panaceas. *Proceedings of the National Academy of Sciences of the United States of America, 104*, 15176–15178. doi:10.1073/pnas0701886104

Parker, J., & Crona, B. (2012). On being all things to all people: Boundary organizations and the contemporary research university. *Social Studies of Science, 42*(2), 262–289.

Perloff, R. M. (2015). Mass communication research at the crossroads: Definitional issues and theoretical directions for mass and political communication scholarship in an age of online media. *Mass Communication and Society, 18*(5), 531–556.

Pohl, C. (2008). From science to policy through transdisciplinary research. *Environmental Science & Policy, 11*(1), 46–53.

Pomeranz, E. F., Decker, D. J., Siemer, W. F., Kirsch, A., Hurst, J., & Farquhar, J. (2014). Challenges for multilevel stakeholder engagement in public trust resource governance. *Human Dimensions of Wildlife, 19*(5), 448–457. doi:10.1080/10871209.2014.936069

Price, V., Tewksbury, D., & Powers, E. (1997). Switching trains of thought: The impact of news frames on readers' cognitive responses. *Communication Research, 24*, 481–506.

Ramachandra, A., & Naha Abu Mansor, N. (2014). Sustainability of community engagement – in the hands of stakeholders? *Education + Training, 56*(7), 588–598. doi:10.1108/ET-07-2014-0084

Reich, S., & Reich, J. (2006). Cultural competence in interdisciplinary Collaborations: A method for respecting diversity in research partnerships. *American Journal of Community Psychology, 38*, 1–7.

Sandman, P. M., Weinstein, N. D., & Klotz, M. L. (1987). Public response to the risk from geological radon. *Journal of Communication, 37*(3), 93–108.

Sigal, L. V. (1973). *Reporters and officials: The organization and politics of newsmaking.* Lexington, MA: D.C. Heath.

Smith, C. (1993). News sources and power elites in news coverage of the Exxon Valdez oil spill. *Journalism & Mass Communication Quarterly, 70*(2), 393–403.

Smith, H. M., & Lindenfeld, L. (2014). Integrating media studies of climate change into transdisciplinary research: Which direction should we be heading? *Environmental Communication, 8*(2), 179–196.

Smith, H. M., & Norton, T. (2013). Environmental groups on par with government sources. *Newspaper Research Journal, 34*(1), 50–61.

Soroka, S. N. (2002). Issue attributes and agenda-setting by media, the public, and policymakers in Canada. *International Journal of Public Opinion Research, 14*(3), 264–285.

Su, L. Y.-F., Akin, H., Brossard, D., Scheufele, D. A., & Xenos, M. A. (2015). Science news consumption patterns and their implications for public understanding of science. *Journalism & Mass Communication Quarterly*, 1077699015586415. doi:10.1177/1077699015586415

Susarla, A. (2003). Plague and arsenic: Assignment of blame in the mass media and the social amplification and attenuation of risk. In N. Pidgeon & R. E. Kasperson (Eds.), *The social amplification of risk* (pp. 179–206). New York, NY: Cambridge University Press.

Tewksbury, D., & Scheufele, D. A. (2009). Media effects: Advances in theory and research. In J. O. Bryant & M. B. Oliver (Eds.), *News framing theory and research* (pp. 17–33). New York, NY: Routledge.

Thuiller, W., Lavorel, S., Araujo, M. B., Sykes, M. T., & Prentice, I. C. (2005). Climate change threats to plant diversity in Europe. *Proceedings of the National Academy of Sciences, 102*(23), 8245–8250. doi:10.1073/pnas.0409902102

Tolman, E. C. (1932). *Purposive behavior in animals and men.* New York, NY: Appleton-Century-Crofts.

Tolman, E. C. (1948). Cognitive maps in rats and men. *The Psychological Review, 55,* 189–208.

Toumey, C. (1996). *Conjuring science: Scientific symbols and cultural meanings in American life.* New Brunswick, NJ: Rutgers University Press.

Tresch, A., Sciarini, P., & Varone, F. (2013). The relationship between media and political agendas: Variations across decision-making phases. *West European Politics, 36,* 897–918. doi:10.1080/01402382.2013.799312

Trumbo, C. (1995). Longitudinal modelling of public issues: An application of the agenda-setting process to the issue of global warming. *Journalism and Mass Communication Monographs, 152.*

Tuchman, G. (1978). *Making news: A study in the construction of reality.* New York, NY: Free Press.

Uzelgun, M. A., & Castro, P. (2015). Climate change in the mainstream Turkish press: Coverage trends and meaning dimensions in the first attention cycle. *Mass Communication & Society, 18*(6), 730–752. doi: 10.1080/15205436.2015.1027407

van Kerkhoff, L., & Lebel, L. (2006). Linking knowledge and action for sustainable development. *Annual Review of Environment & Resources, 31*(1), 445–477.

Weaver, D., Graber, D. A., McCombs, M. E., & Eyal, C. H. (1981). *Media agenda-setting in a presidential election: Issues, images, and interest.* New York, NY: Praeger.

Weerts, D. J., & Sandmann, L. R. (2010, November 01). Community engagement and boundary-spanning roles at research universities. *Journal of Higher Education, 81*(6), 702–727.

West, B., Sandman, P. M., & Greenberg, M. R. (1995). *The reporter's environmental handbook.* New Brunswick, NJ: Rutgers University Press.

Yeo, T. (2014). Negotiating virtue and vice: Articulations of lay conceptions of health and sustainability in social media conversations around natural beverages. *Environmental Communication, 8* (1), 39–57.

Zucker, H. G. (1978). The variable nature of news media influence. In B. D. Ruben (Ed.), *Communication yearbook 2* (pp. 225–240). New Brunswick, NJ: Transaction Books.

Who Is Responsible for Climate Change? Attribution of Responsibility, News Media, and South Koreans' Perceived Risk of Climate Change

Jeongheon JC Chang

Department of Health & Strategic Communication
Cha University

Sei-Hill Kim

School of Journalism and Mass Communications
University of South Carolina

Jae Chul Shim and Dong Hoon Ma

School of Media & Communication
Korea University

Analyzing data from a survey of South Koreans' perceptions of climate change, this study examines whether the way people attribute responsibility can affect their perceived risks. We also examine the role of the media in this process, looking at whether media use can influence the way the audiences attribute responsibility. Our findings provided support for the basic principles of risk perception that perceived controllability of a risk can affect the level of perceived risk (Slovic, Fischhoff, & Lichtenstein, 1982). Respondents who believed that the government or large corporations—as opposed to average citizens—were responsible for the negative consequences of climate change indicated perceptions of a greater risk because the risk was believed to be beyond their own control and determined largely by another entity (i.e., the government or corporations). When it comes to the role of the media, television news viewing was negatively associated with attributing responsibility to the government and to large corporations. On the contrary, uses of online bulletin boards and blogs were positively associated with blaming the government and corporations. By assessing the role of attribution in perceiving climate change risk, this study adds a new and likely helpful discovery regarding the dynamics of climate change perceptions.

For decades, South Korea has fully experienced the impacts of rapid climate change. The average temperature in the country has increased 1.5 °C over the last 100 years, which represents twice the global average of 0.74 °C (Lee & Oh, 2010). When compared to the 1920s, the winter weather has decreased by around 30 days, whereas the spring and summer weather has increased by around 20 days (The Government of the Republic of Korea, 2003). Climate change has been a prominent issue in South Korea, and the public seems to perceive relatively greater risks, compared to people in other countries. According to the 2010 Pew Global Attitudes Project poll (Pew Research Center, 2010), about 68% of South Koreans believed that global warming was a *very serious* problem, which was fourth highest among the 23 countries surveyed. The average of the 23 countries was 53%, and only about 37% of American respondents believed the same. South Koreans also tend to believe that the government is highly responsible for addressing the issue of climate change. In the 2009 World Public Opinion poll (Program on International Policy Attitudes, 2009), about 81% of South Koreans answered that the government should place a higher priority on addressing climate change than it did. This number (81%) was the highest among the 22 countries surveyed; only 52% of the respondents in the United States, for example, answered that the government should place a higher priority.

With this great public concern, there have been increasing conversations about climate change not only among policymakers but also among the citizens and mass media in South Korea (Lee & Oh, 2010). At the center of the conversations is the question of who is responsible for climate change. As Nisbet (2014) pointed out, defining who is responsible has been one of the key talking points when discussing many environmental issues including climate change. How to define responsibility is important for many reasons; most important, it can help dictate the direction of efforts to bring about change (Kim, Tanner, Foster, & Kim, 2015; Kim & Willis, 2007). To a certain extent, how to define responsibility can either extend or constrain the policy options available to address a given problem (Stone, 1989).

The present study examines another important outcome of attributing responsibility. In our study, attribution of responsibility refers to the extent to which one finds an entity responsible for potential negative consequences of climate change. We examine whether there is a significant correlation between attribution of responsibility and risk perception. More specifically, we theorize that the way a person attributes responsibility can affect his or her perceived level of potential risk associated with climate change. For example, we hypothesize that those who believe that climate change is in large part an outcome of the government's inability to adequately address the problem—as opposed to an outcome of irresponsible activities of average citizens like themselves—will perceive a greater risk because the risk is perceived to be beyond their own control and determined largely by another entity (i.e., the government).

We focus on large corporations, the government, and average citizens as the primary entities who can potentially be held responsible for climate change (Heede, 2014). Large corporations—major carbon-emitting industries, in particular—are one of the most direct and immediate sources of the problem. National and local governments are responsible in a sense that they have the authority to oversee and regulate the carbon-producing industries. Average citizens are also responsible through their daily activities from purchasing environment-friendly consumer products to volunteering to defend communities against climate impacts (Nisbet, 2014). Using data collected from an online survey of respondents in South Korea, this study examines whether the extent to which a person attributes responsibility to these three entities is related with his or her perceived risk of climate change.

We then look into the role of news media in shaping the audience's conception of who is responsible. The media have been found to play an important role in defining or *framing* a social problem by diagnosing the causes and suggesting potential remedies (Entman, 1993; Kim, Carvalho, & Davis, 2010). In this way, the media can lead the audiences to make attributions of responsibility, telling them who is responsible for causing and solving a given problem (Iyengar, 1991). Do South Korea news media affect the way the audiences attribute responsibility for climate change? This study examines whether individuals' use of news media for science information is associated with the extent to which they attribute responsibility to themselves, to the government, and to large corporations.

Our study can make several unique contributions to the environmental and risk communication literatures. First, little research, with only a few exceptions (e.g., Kahlor, Dunwoody, & Griffin, 2002; Sellström, Bremberg, Gärling, & Hörnquist, 2000), has examined the potential link between attribution of responsibility and risk perception. This gap in research is somewhat surprising given that the question of who is responsible is one of the central talking points in discussing many social problems and risks (Entman, 1993; Nisbet, 2014). Using the issue of climate change, our study tests a new theorization that links attribution of responsibility to perceived risks among the public. Second, by providing data from South Korea, this study can expand our intercultural understanding of the role of environmental and risk communications. Although the link between communication—mass media use in particular—and the public's perceptions of climate change has produced significant attention among researchers in Europe and North America, relatively less research has been carried out in Asian countries. Given the great public concern about climate change, South Korea can offer a unique opportunity to enhance the intercultural validity of the previous findings and theorizing from the science communication literature.

ATTRIBUTION OF RESPONSIBILITY AND RISK PERCEPTION

Researchers of *attribution theory* (Weiner, 1993, 1995) have examined a number of social- and individual-level outcomes of responsibility attribution. Within a societal context, researchers have explored how social attribution of responsibility affects the policy options for addressing a given problem (e.g., Kim, Carvalho, Davis, & Mullins, 2011). More specifically, prior research has investigated whether the way people attribute responsibility can affect their support for certain government policies. A good amount of research, for example, demonstrated that attribution of responsibility (to victims vs. to uncontrollable external factors) was significantly associated with one's support for government aid programs, such as welfare (Iyengar, 1990) and federal disaster assistance (Skitka, 1999). When it comes to the issue of climate change, a few studies (e.g., Jang, 2013; Taylor, Dessai, & de Bruin, 2014) found that the way the public attributed responsibility (to nature vs. to humans vs. to the government) was significantly correlated with the level of support for global- and domestic-level climate change policies.

At an individual level, studies have examined a number of emotional and behavioral outcomes of responsibility attribution. According to Weiner's (1993) theorization, these three concepts are interrelated in a sense that attributing responsibility (to victims vs. to uncontrollable external factors) can affect one's emotions (e.g., sympathy, anger), which in turn can lead to certain behaviors (help giving, aggression, or peer rejection). Prior research has demonstrated that attribution of responsibility is significantly associated with expressions of pity and anger (e.g., Hamann, Howell, & McDonald, 2013), willingness to help (e.g., Jones & Ruthig, 2014), peer rejection (e.g., Juvonen, 1992), and aggression (e.g., Graham, Hudley, & Williams, 1992).

Far less research has been devoted to investigating potential outcomes of responsibility attribution in terms of risk perception. Our study attempts to examine whether the way a person attributes responsibility (to themselves, to the government, to corporations) can affect his or her perceived level of risk associated with climate change. How can attribution of responsibility affect one's estimate of a potential risk? We focus on the notion of *perceived controllability* as an important component of risk perception (Slovic, Fischhoff, & Lichtenstein, 1982). As Weinstein (1980) explained, people tend to perceive a greater probability of a positive outcome when they feel they are more in control of a situation, whereas they perceive a greater risk when the risk is perceived to be beyond their own control. It is therefore hypothesized that those who believe that the government or large corporations—as opposed to average citizens like themselves—are highly responsible for producing the negative consequences of climate change will perceive a *greater* risk because the risk is perceived to be beyond their own control and determined largely by another entity (i.e., the government or corporations). In this context, we also hypothesize that those who attribute greater responsibility to themselves will perceive a *lower* level of risk because they believe that there is much they themselves can do to control or reduce the risk of climate change.

Research has demonstrated that perceptions of greater controllability were associated with lower levels of perceived risk. Drivers, for example, tend to perceive a greater risk of car accident when they believe that most accidents are caused by the fault of other drivers (i.e., risk is less controllable), rather than by their own fault (DeJoy, 1989). Similarly, drivers in general tend to feel more comfortable with faster speeds than passengers because those who are in control (drivers) perceive lower levels of risk compared to those who are not (passengers; Horswill & McKenna, 1999). In the context of an environmental risk, Ho, Shaw, Lin, and Chiu (2008) also found that those who thought themselves to be largely incapable of controlling the risk of landslide perceived a greater potential impact of landslide than those who thought otherwise. We theorize that the way people attribute responsibility (to themselves vs. to external factors) are related with their perceived controllability of a risk in such a way that attributing responsibility to external factors (such as the government or large corporations) is correlated with lower levels of perceived controllability, which in turn will lead to perceptions of a greater risk. Supporting this line of reasoning, a few studies have demonstrated that attribution of responsibility is associated with perceived risk (Gärling, 1988; Sellström et al., 2000). In a study of mothers' perceived risk of children's burn injury, for example, Sellström et al. (2000) found that those who attributed greater responsibility to the environment—as opposed to mothers themselves—perceived a greater risk of burn injury. We put forth the following hypotheses:

H1a: Those who attribute greater responsibility to themselves will perceive lower risks associated with climate change.

H1b: Those who attribute greater responsibility to the government will perceive higher risks associated with climate change.

H1c: Those who attribute greater responsibility to corporations will perceive higher risks associated with climate change.

We also test a potential interaction between attribution of responsibility and institutional trust in affecting risk perception. When the government is believed to be largely in control of the climate change risk, for example, we hypothesize that perceived risk will be lower among those who have much trust in the government because they believe that the government will take good care of the problem. That is, the influence of responsibility attribution on risk perception will be smaller among those who have much trust in the government. On the other hand, those who trust the government less will perceive a greater risk because they may have little confidence in the government's ability to adequately address the problem. Therefore, the influence of attributing responsibility to the government will be greater among those who have less trust. Similarly, we examine whether trust in corporations also can moderate the relationship between attributing responsibility to large corporations and perceived risk. We test the following hypotheses:

H2a: The correlation between perceived government responsibility and risk perception will be greater among those who have less trust in the government.

H2b: The correlation between perceived corporate responsibility and risk perception will be greater among those who have less trust in corporations.

MEDIA USE AND PERCEIVED RESPONSIBILITY

As Brossard and Nisbet (2007) pointed out, mass media might be the most available and often times the only source from which the public obtains information about scientific discoveries and controversies. More importantly, mass media also can help audiences construct their views on whom should be held responsible for the problems associated with scientific controversies (Priest, 2001). It is, therefore, likely that the media can play an important role in shaping the public's perceptions of who is responsible for the potential risks of climate change. Nevertheless, there has been little research on how the media discuss the question of responsibility in their presentation of environmental or climate change issues. Another important but under-researched question is whether the media can affect the audiences' perceptions of who should be held responsible for the environmental problems.

In this study, we examine whether individuals' use of the media for science information is associated with their perceptions of whom is responsible for climate change. Using four news sources (newspapers, television news, online newspapers, and online bulletin boards and blogs), more specifically, we investigate whether the amount of individuals' science media use is correlated with the extent to which they attribute responsibility to themselves, to the government, and to large corporations. To our knowledge, there has been no systemic content-analysis research on how the question of responsibility is discussed in South Korean media's presentation of the issue of climate change. We thus propose a research question instead of testing a formal hypothesis:

RQ1: What is the relationship like between science media use and attribution of responsibility?

METHODS

Sample

Data for this study were collected in South Korea in August 2011, as part of the Korea Food and Drug Administration's annual survey of the public's perceptions of a variety of health issues. A nationwide online survey firm recruited the respondents from a panel of about 650,000 potential participants. Sampling was done via a nonprobability quota sampling method, based on respondents' age, gender, and geographical regions. Based on the quotas, e-mail solicitations were sent out to the potential respondents who met the criteria. Participants then were instructed that the survey would be confidential and that they were allowed to withdraw from the survey at any time. Individuals could not participate once the subgroup (age, gender, regions) quota had been reached. This means we were not able to calculate a meaningful response rate. The purpose of our sampling design was to ensure representative diversity in terms of gender, age groups, and geographical regions. The survey process closely followed Korea University's protocols for doing research with human subjects.

Measurements

Unlike other risk factors (such as cigarette smoking), potential consequences of climate change can affect anyone, whether or not they engage in a certain behavior (such as cigarette smoking). It is also likely that the public perceives the effects of climate change to be long term and delayed rather than short term or immediate. Therefore, respondents' *perceived risk of climate change* was measured in terms of its effects not only on the respondents themselves but also on other people and the next generation. Respondents were asked to rate, from 1 (*not at all risky*) to 7 (*very risky*), how risky they perceived the consequences of climate change would be (a) to themselves, (b) to others, and (c) to the next generation. *Attribution of responsibility* also was measured with three items. On a 7-point scale from 1 (*not at all responsible*) to 7 (*very responsible*), respondents were asked how much they perceived responsibility for potential negative consequences of climate change lay with (a) respondents themselves, (b) government, and (c) larger corporations.

Respondents' *science media use* was measured against the amounts of exposure and attention to science and health information on (a) newspapers, (b) television news, (c) online newspapers, and (d) online bulletin boards and blogs. We used two questions tapping how often, from 1 (*never*) to 10 (*very often*) respondents viewed and how much attention, from 1 (*none*) to 10 (*very much*), they paid to each medium. These two exposure and attention measures were combined into a single variable representing the amount of using each medium for science and health information: newspapers ($r = .721$), television news ($r = .731$), online newspapers ($r = .755$), and online bulletin boards and blogs ($r = .783$).

Two measures of institutional *trust* assessed respondents' general trust in the government and large corporations. Respondents were asked how much in general, from 1 (*not at all*) to 5 (*very much*), they trust the government ($M = 2.61$, $SD = .89$) and large corporations ($M = 2.40$, $SD = .86$). For control purposes, respondents' ideology and perceived uncertainty were assessed. *Ideology* was measured on a simple conservative–liberal scale from 1 (*very conservative*) to 5 (*very liberal; M = 2.02, SD = .57*). *Uncertainty* was measured by asking respondents' perceptions of how well potential risks of climate change were known to the public, from 1 (*not well known*) to 7 (*well known*, reverse-coded; $M = 4.80$, $SD = 1.36$). Demographic controls included gender (50% female), age ($M = 41.49$, $SD = 13.02$), education (the highest degree completed, 64.0% with college diploma or more), and family income (*Mdn* household monthly income = 3–4 million Korean Won [about US$3,000–$4,000]].

FINDINGS

Before introducing findings regarding our proposed hypotheses and research question, we first report some descriptive statistics of the key variables to give non-Korean readers a good sense of the public's perceptions of climate change and science media use in South Korea. Findings in Table 1 report the levels of perceived risks associated with climate change. Perceived risk to the next generation ($M = 5.83$) approached 6 on the 7-point scale, suggesting that the

TABLE 1
Descriptive Statistics

Variables	M (SD)
Perceived risk of climate change (1 = *not at all risky*; 7 = *very risky*)	
to self	5.00 (1.29)
to others	5.17 (1.25)
to the next generation	5.83 (1.30)
Attribution of responsibility (1 = *not at all responsible*; 7 = *very responsible*)	
to self	3.36 (1.72)
to the government	4.48 (1.64)
to corporations	4.01 (1.64)
Science media use (additive index of exposure [1 = *never*; 10 = *very often*]) and attention [1 = *none*; 10 = *very much*] measures)	
Newspapers	11.13 (3.92)
Television news	13.44 (3.28)
Online newspapers	12.87 (3.91)
Online bulletin boards and blogs	11.65 (4.24)

Note. N = 1,001.

perceived risk is quite substantial. Perceived risk to self had the lowest mean score (M = 5.00), but the score still was higher than the midpoint (4) of the scale. A series of *paired-samples t tests* indicated that the risk to the next generation was perceived significantly higher than the risks to self (t = 17.23, p < .001) and others (t = 13.83, p < .001). South Koreans seem to perceive that climate change is more of a problem tomorrow than it is today.

When it comes to who is responsible for climate change, our respondents were most likely to attribute responsibility to the government (M = 4.48), followed by large corporations (M = 4.01) and themselves (M = 3.36). Again, a series of *paired-samples t tests* confirmed that the responsibility of the government was perceived as significantly greater than that of respondents themselves (t = 25.62, p < .001) and corporations (t = 9.44, p < .001). It is interesting that the government's responsibility to oversee the issue and to regulate large corporations is perceived to be greater than the responsibility of the corporations themselves, who are in fact one of the most direct and immediate sources of the problem.

Table 1 also reports South Koreans' uses of media for science and health information. Television news indicated the highest mean score (M = 13.44), followed by online newspapers (M = 12.87), online bulletin boards and blogs (M = 11.65), and newspapers (M = 11.13). Use of television news was significantly greater than uses of online newspapers (t = 4.59, p < .001), online bulletin boards and blogs ($t = 11.95$, $p < .001$), and newspapers ($t = 18.69$, $p < .001$), suggesting that television news, among the media outlets examined, is the most heavily used source of science and health information in South Korea.

Our hypotheses were tested using hierarchical regression (ordinary least squares), where three measures of perceived risk (to self, to others, to the next generation) were regressed onto a series of hypothesized independent variables (see Table 2). For control purposes, respondents' demographics (gender, age, education, family income) entered the regression first. Respondents' political ideology and perceived uncertainty also entered regression because research has

TABLE 2
Predicting Risk Perceptions

	Perceived Risk of Climate Change		
	to Self	to Others	to the Next Generation
Control variables			
Gender (female)	.074*	.063*	.089**
Age	.078*	.068*	−.005
Education	.013	.011	.060
Family income	.059	.032	−.015
Ideology	.016	−.006	.039
uncertainty	.237***	.280***	.169***
Incremental R^2 (%)	9.5***	11.8***	6.4***
Institutional trust			
Trust in the government	.023	.011	.016
Trust in corporations	−.008	−.026	−.096**
Incremental R^2 (%)	.0	.1	.6
Science media use			
Newspapers	−.024	−.053	.042
Television news	.044	.084*	.097**
Online newspapers	.045	.045	.072
Online bulletin boards and blogs	.011	.012	−.004
Incremental R^2 (%)	.6	1.0*	2.4***
Attribution of responsibility			
to self	.046	−.012	.059
to the government	.110**	.172***	.096**
to corporations	.101**	.096**	.083*
Incremental R^2 (%)	4.1***	5.3***	3.4***
Interactions			
Government Responsibility × Trust	−.122***	−.065*	−.051
Corporate Responsibility × Trust	.052	.010	−.008
Incremental R^2 (%)	1.4***	.4	.3
Total R^2 (%)	15.6***	18.6***	13.0***

Note. $N = 1,001$. Entries are standardized regression coefficients (final betas).
*$p < .05$. **$p < .01$. ***$p < .001$.

33

reported that ideology (Leiserowitz, 2006; McCright & Dunlap, 2011) and uncertainty (Spence, Poortinga, & Pidgeon, 2012) are important predictors of the public's estimates of risks associated with climate change. Two measures of institutional trust (trust in the government and trust in corporations) were a component of two interaction terms (Government Responsibility × Trust and Corporate Responsibility × Trust) to be tested, and thus entered regression in the next step to test their *main effects*. Science media uses (newspapers, television news, online newspapers, online bulletin boards and blogs) were then entered into regression before two blocks of the key independent variables—attributions of responsibility (to self, to the government, to corporations) and the interaction terms—entered regression in the final steps. Entries in Table 2 report final betas (β) estimated after all variables entered the regression.

Our first three hypotheses (H1a, H1b, H1c) examine whether attribution of responsibility (to self, to the government, to corporations) is related to the level of perceived risk. Findings in Table 2 show that attributing responsibility to self was largely unrelated with perceived risk measures: to self (β = .046, *ns*), to others (β = −.012, *ns*), to the next generation (β = .059, *ns*). H1a was not supported. Attribution of responsibility to the government, on the other hand, had a positive and significant relationship to all three measures of perceived risk: to self (β = .110, $p < .01$), to others (β = .172, $p < .001$), to the next generation (β = .096, $p < .01$), indicating that those who attribute greater responsibility to the government tend to perceive greater risk. H1b was supported. H1c was supported as well. As shown in Table 2, attributing responsibility to corporations was positively and significantly associated with perceived risk to self (β = .101, $p < .01$), to others (β = .096, $p < .01$), and to the next generation (β = .083, $p < .05$). Those who attribute greater responsibility to large corporations seem to perceive greater risk.

Our next two hypotheses (H2a, H2b) test the moderating role of institutional trust (trust in the government, trust in corporations), looking at whether institutional trust moderates the correlation between responsibility attribution and perceived risk. The moderating role was tested using a moderated multiple regression method, which entered two interaction terms (Government Responsibility × Trust in the Government, Corporate Responsibility × Trust in Corporations) along with their main-effect terms (see Table 2). Moderated multiple regression uses continuous (as opposed to dichotomous) measures of both the independent and the moderator variables in producing an interaction term (Cohen & Cohen, 1983). To minimize multicollinearity between the components of an interaction term and the interaction term itself, attribution of responsibility and institutional trust measures were all *z*-standardized before entering the regression (Dunlap & Kemery, 1987).

As shown in Table 2, attributing responsibility to the government indicated a significant interaction with trust in the government in predicting one's perceived risk to himself/herself (β = −.122, $p < .001$) and to others (β = −.065, $p < .05$). To further examine these interactions, we compared regression coefficients (β) of attributing responsibility to the government among respondents with high ($M = 3$ or higher) and low ($M =$ less than 3) trust in the government (not shown in Table 2). In predicting perceived risk to self, the regression coefficient was considerably greater among low-trust respondents ($\beta = .261$, $p < .001$) than it was among high-trust respondents ($\beta = -.016$, ns). When predicting perceived risk to others, again, the coefficient among low-trust respondents ($\beta = .268$, $p < .001$) was greater than the coefficient among high-trust respondents ($\beta = .094$, $p < .05$). Supporting H2a, these findings suggest that the correlation between perceived government responsibility and perceived risk (to self, to others) is greater among those who have less trust in the government. When it comes to attributing responsibility to corporations (see Table 2), however, none of the three interaction terms were statistically significant (to self: $\beta = .052$, ns; to others: $\beta = .010$, ns; to the next generation: $\beta = -.008$, ns). H2b was not supported in this study.

RQ1 questions how individuals' use of science media is related with perceptions of who is responsible for climate change. More specifically, we examine whether the use of science media is related to the extent to which they attribute responsibility to themselves, to the government, and to large corporations. The relationships between science media use and attribution of responsibility was examined using another hierarchical regression (ordinary least squares), where three measures of attribution of responsibility (to self, to the government, to corporations) were regressed onto science media use and other control variables (see Table 3). Four measures of science media use (newspapers, television news, online newspapers, online bulletin board and blogs) entered regression after control (gender, age, education, family income, ideology, uncertainty) and institutional trust variables (trust in the government, trust in corporations).

Findings in Table 3 show that television news and online bulletin board and blogs can play an important role in shaping perceptions of the government's and corporations' responsibility for climate change. Using television news for science and health information was negatively and significantly associated with attributing responsibility to the government ($\beta = -.099$, $p < .05$) and to corporations ($\beta = -.129$, $p < .01$), indicating that those with greater exposure and attention to television news were *less* likely to attribute responsibility to the government or to corporations. Online bulletin board and blogs, on the other hand, showed significant positive relationships, suggesting that that those with greater exposure and attention to online bulletin board and blogs were *more* likely to attribute responsibility to the government ($\beta = .089$, $p < .05$) or to corporations ($\beta = .199$, $p < .001$).

TABLE 3
Predicting Attribution of Responsibility

	Attribution of Responsibility		
	to Self	to the Government	to Corporations
Control variables			
Gender (female)	−.017	−.042	−.032
Age	−.076*	.017	−.001
Education	.025	.019	.032
Family income	−.013	−.031	−.008
Ideology	−.057	.021	−.028
Uncertainty	.052	.114***	.050
Incremental R^2 (%)	1.4*	1.70**	.600
Trust			
Trust in the government	−.001	−.079*	−.134***
Trust in corporations	.106**	.011	.081*
Incremental R^2 (%)	1.20**	.600	1.5***
Science media use			
Newspapers	.018	.029	.022
Television news	−.038	−.099*	−.129**
Online newspapers	.040	.018	−.051
Online bulletin boards and blogs	.049	.089*	.199***
Incremental R^2 (%)	.600	1.3**	3.8***
Total R^2 (%)	3.1**	3.6***	5.9***

Note. $N = 1,001$. Entries are standardized regression coefficients (final betas).
$*p < .05.$ $**p < .01.$ $***p < .001.$

DISCUSSION

Analyzing data from an online survey of respondents in South Korea, this study examined how attribution of responsibility could be linked to the public's perceived risk of climate change. The present study also examined what role the media could play in shaping the audiences' understanding of who should be held responsible for climate change and its negative consequences. Our measurements of perceived risks ranged between about 5 (risk to self) and 6 (risk to the next generation) on a 7-point scale, indicating that perceived risks of climate change among South Koreans are quite substantial. We also found that South Koreans held the government most responsible, followed by large corporations and average citizens like themselves, suggesting that climate change is thought to be an outcome of the government's inability to adequately address the problem, rather than an outcome of average citizens' irresponsible activities.

These attributions of responsibility had a small but statistically significant relationship with risk perception. Attributing greater responsibility to the government was associated with perceptions of greater risks to self, to others, and to the next generation. Attributing responsibility to large corporations was also associated with perceptions of greater risks, suggesting that those who believe that the government and large corporations—as opposed to average citizens—are largely responsible for negative consequences of climate change tend to perceive a greater risk because the risk is perceived to be beyond their own control and determined mostly by another entity. Attributing responsibility to self, however, was unrelated to risk perception, though we hypothesized a negative correlation. Our findings also indicated that institutional trust could moderate the correlation between attribution of responsibility and perceived risks. In predicting perceived risks to self and to others, the influence of attributing responsibility to the government was greater among those who have less trust in the government.

The role of viewing television news was pronounced in our study. According to our data, television news was the most heavily used medium for science and health information in South Korea. At the same time, television news viewing was *negatively* and significantly associated with attributing responsibility to the government and to large corporations. On the contrary, uses of online bulletin boards and blogs were *positively* associated with blaming the government and corporations for climate change. Why is viewing television news negatively correlated with attributing responsibility, whereas using online bulletin boards and blogs has positive correlations? One of our survey questions may *hint* why these two news sources can have two opposite influences. The survey question asked respondents to rate, on a 10-point scale, how favorably or unfavorably different news outlets portrayed the government's performance in addressing science and health issues. Of the four news sources examined (newspapers, television news, online newspapers, online bulletin board and blogs), television news was rated most favorable ($M = 5.33$), whereas online bulletin boards and blogs were rated least favorable ($M = 4.57$). By presenting the government in a positive light in news coverage of climate change, television might have affected the viewers to become less likely to attribute responsibility to the government. On the other hand, the relatively unfavorable presentation in online bulletin boards and blogs might have led the users to become more likely to blame the government.

Before further discussing our findings, it is necessary to point out several limitations of our study. First, we have to question whether the explanatory power we estimated was substantial enough to support a new theorization. The correlation (regression beta) between attribution of responsibility and risk perception only ranged between .083 and .172, and the three measures of responsibility attribution accounted for only about 3.4% to 5.3% of the variance in risk perception (see Table 2). The relatively small explanatory power can suggest that the effect of responsibility attribution is *indeed* small. At the same time, however, the small effect sizes can be attributed to our use of imprecise measurements. In particular, our operationalization of the key variables (attributions of responsibility and risk perceptions) was all based on single-item measures, which raises concern about their reliability and content validity (i.e., how exhaustively a given set of indicators measures a given construct). Despite these apparent limitations, the lack of multiple measures in our secondary data set limited us to using the single-item measures. Given these limitations in measurements, it is important to point out that our study is largely exploratory, and the findings should be considered as preliminary at best, to be further validated only in future studies using multiple measurement items with enhanced reliability and validity.

Second, the cross-sectional nature of our data limits our ability to make a strong inference about causal direction. The significant correlation between attribution of responsibility and risk perception can be interpreted as indicating that attribution of responsibility, as hypothesized, can affect risk perception. The same correlation, however, also can indicate a reverse-causation that the level of perceived risk can affect the way a person attributes responsibility. In particular, studies on environmental risk perception (e.g., Rickard, Yang, Seo, & Harrison, 2014) have demonstrated that people tend to attribute negative outcomes (higher risk) to external factors while attributing positive outcomes (lower risk) to internal factors, which can produce a positive correlation between perceived risk and attributing responsibility to an external factor, such as the government. At the same time, the relationship can be reciprocal, that is, attributions of responsibility and risk perceptions influence each other (Kahlor et al., 2002). When interpreting our findings, therefore, we should not rule out the possibility of opposite causal direction, and the ambiguity of causal direction reminds us not to overinterpret the hypothesized effects of responsibility attribution on risk perception. Future research building on our findings needs to use longitudinal or experimental data to further establish the time-order effect.

Finally, we have to point out that our proposed causal mechanism remains largely untested. We theorized that those who believed that climate change was in most part an outcome of the government's or corporations' inability to address the problem would perceive a greater risk because they would believe that the risk was beyond their own control and determined largely by another entity (i.e., the government or corporations). In other words, we suggest that it is, perceived controllability of the risk that links attribution of responsibility to risk perception. This *mediating* role of perceived controllability, however, was simply a theoretical assumption and was not tested with data in this study. Again, our use of a secondary data set limited us to only the variables available in the data set. Nevertheless, the significant interaction between attribution of responsibility and institutional trust can support at least *indirectly* our proposed causal mechanism (i.e., the mediating role of perceived controllability). The significant interaction can suggest that attributing responsibility to the government has a smaller influence among those with higher trust in the government because they believe that the government is largely *in control* of the risk and that the government will take care of the problem. Even though this significant interaction does not rule out the possibility of other causal interpretations, it may enhance the validity of our causal claim that perceived controllability can mediate the link between attribution of responsibility and risk perception.

With these shortcomings in mind, our findings can have a number of theoretical implications. As Nisbet (2014) pointed out, the question of who is responsible is an important component of communicating environmental and other risks. Although potential outcomes of responsibility attribution have been studied in a variety of context, its influence on risk perception rarely has been examined in empirical investigations (Rickard et al., 2014). In this study, we proposed new ways of theorizing to explain how attribution of responsibility might affect perceived risk, particularly in the context of an environmental risk.

Our findings can aid future researchers who hope to more thoroughly understand perceptions of climate change risk. First, the role of perceived controllability in determining perceived risks (Slovic et al., 1982) is highlighted in this study. In our theorization, perceived controllability not only affects risk perception directly but also *mediates* the link between attribution of responsibility and risk perception (attribution of responsibility → perceived controllability → risk perception). Given that this mediating role was not actually tested in this study, future research needs to examine in an empirical investigation whether attribution of responsibility is indeed related to perceived controllability, which in turn can affect risk perception. At the same time, it is unlikely that perceived controllability is the only mediator that connects responsibility attribution to risk perception. Future research, for example, can examine whether finding the government or corporations responsible for climate change can produce negative emotions—such as anger and fear—which have been found to influence one's assessment of potential risks (e.g., Loewenstein, Weber, Hsee, & Welch, 2001). Second, we found that institutional trust could *moderate* the influence of responsibility attribution on risk perception, suggesting that institutional trust can be an important component of risk communication (Groothuis & Miller, 1997). Although the direct correlation between institutional trust and risk perception often has been investigated (e.g., Priest, 2001), our findings provide another important explanation of how institutional trust can play a role in shaping risk perceptions. Our data indicate that finding the government responsible may not necessarily mean people perceive significant risk so long as they have trust in government.

Findings in this study also can contribute to the media effects literature by demonstrating the role of the media in shaping audiences' perceptions of who is responsible. Although this particular role has often been examined in the previous literature (e.g., Iyengar, 1991), our study is one of the first attempts to link this role to risk perception. We found that media may influence the audiences' attributions of responsibility, which, in turn, affected risk perception. The media effects being mediated by attribution of responsibility can be another important role the media can play in communicating environmental risks. By questioning the government's or corporations' ability and willingness to deal with climate change, the media seem to increase, rather than reduce, perceived risks among the audiences.

The potential links between the media, attribution of responsibility, and risk perception can offer new opportunities to generate more sophisticated hypotheses than those previously advanced, and our study may provide routes for new theorizing that can make a significant contribution. First, future research needs to investigate specifically what kinds of content in the media can affect the audiences' attributions of responsibility for climate change. Although we explained that the favorable portrayals of the government in television and the unfavorable portrayals in online bulletin boards and blogs might have affected the audiences' perceived responsibility, these explanations are largely speculative. Researchers may find the content analysis research method useful for identifying the specific content responsible for producing such a media effect. Future research also needs to incorporate a variety of digital media in investigating climate change communication. As the spread of social media and mobile technology is rapidly adding to media consumption (Pew Research Center, 2012), it seems necessary to examine how climate change is discussed in the ever-growing assortment of digital news sources, and whether such discussions can affect the users' attribution of responsibility and risk perceptions.

Understanding perceptions of responsibility for climate change is particularly important for the government and corporations because it can affect the scope and nature of environmental regulations (Jang, 2013; Taylor et al., 2014). At the same time, our findings indicate that the way public attributes responsibility also can affect risk perception. As Ho et al. (2008) pointed out, identifying factors that affect the public's risk perception is essential for designing risk communications and improving mitigation policies, since the government and corporations have a legal and ethical responsibility –or a strategic interest in maintaining a certain level of perceived risk among the public. When it comes to advocacy organizations, our findings suggest that presenting climate change in terms of the government's and corporations' responsibility can be an effective way to increase perceived risk among public, which in turn can lead to greater public support for regulating the carbon-emitting industries. Our findings also demonstrate that the media can be an important tool for communicating about climate change responsibility.

REFERENCES

Brossard, D., & Nisbet, M. (2007). Deference to scientific authority among a low information public understanding U.S. opinion on agricultural biotechnology. *International Journal of Public Opinion Research, 19*, 24–52.

Cohen, J., & Cohen, P. (1983). *Applied multiple regression/correlation analysis for the behavioral sciences* (2nd ed.). Hillsdale, NJ: Erlbaum.

Deloy, D. M. (1989). The optimism bias and traffic accident risk perception. *Accident Analysis & Prevention, 21*, 333–340.

Dunlap, W. P., & Kemery, E. R. (1987). Failure to detect moderating effects: Is multicollinearity the problem? *Psychological Bulletin, 102*, 418–420.

Entman, R. M. (1993). Framing: Toward clarification of a fractured paradigm. *Journal of Communication, 43*, 51–58.

Gärling, A. (1988). Parents perceptions of children's accident risk (Unpublished doctoral dissertation). University of Umea, Umea, Sweden.

Graham, S., Hudley, C., & Williams, E. (1992). Attributional and emotional determinants of aggression among African-American and Latino young adolescents. *Developmental Psychology, 28*, 731–740.

Groothuis, P. A., & Miller, G. (1997). The role of social distrust in risk-benefit analysis: A study of the siting of a hazardous waste disposal facility. *Journal of Risk and Uncertainty, 15*, 241–257.

Hamann, H. A., Howell, L. A., & McDonald, J. L. (2013). Causal attributions and attitudes toward lung cancer. *Journal of Applied Social Psychology, 43*, E37–E45.

Heede, R. (2014). Tracing anthropogenic carbon dioxide and methane emissions to fossil fuel and cement producers, 1854–2010. *Climatic Change, 122*, 229–241.

Ho, M. C., Shaw, D., Lin, S., & Chiu, Y. C. (2008). How do disaster characteristics influence risk perception? *Risk Analysis, 28*, 635–643.

Horswill, M. S., & McKenna, F. P. (1999). The effect of perceived control on risk taking. *Journal of Applied Social Psychology, 29*, 377–391.

Iyengar, S. (1990). Framing responsibility for political issues: The case of poverty. *Political Behavior, 12*, 19–40.

Iyengar, S. (1991). *Is anyone responsible? How television frames political issues*. Chicago, IL, USA: University of Chicago Press.

Jang, S. M. (2013). Framing responsibility in climate change discourse: Ethnocentric attribution bias, perceived causes, and policy attitudes. *Journal of Environmental Psychology, 36*, 27–36.

Jones, K. M., & Ruthig, J. C. (2015). The impact of positive thinking, gender, and empathy on social attributions for cancer outcomes. *Current Psychology, 34*, 762–771.

Juvonen, J. (1992). Negative peer reactions from the perspective of the reactor. *Journal of Educational Psychology, 84*, 314–321.

Kahlor, L., Dunwoody, S., & Griffin, R. J. (2002). Attributions in explanations of risk estimates. *Public Understanding of Science, 11*, 243–257.

Kim, S.-H., Carvalho, J. P., & Davis, A. G. (2010). Talking about poverty: News framing of who is responsible for causing and fixing the problem. *Journalism & Mass Communication Quarterly, 87*, 563–581.

Kim, S.-H., Carvalho, J. P., Davis, A. G., & Mullins, A. M. (2011). The view of the border: News framing of the definition, causes, and solutions to illegal immigration. *Mass Communication & Society, 14*, 292–314.

Kim, S.-H., Tanner, A., Foster, C., & Kim, S. Y. (2015). Talking about healthcare: News framing of who is responsible for rising healthcare costs in the United States. *Journal of Health Communication, 20*, 123–133.

Kim, S.-H., & Willis, L. A. (2007). Talking about obesity: News framing of who is responsible for causing and fixing the problem. *Journal of Health Communication, 12*, 359–376.

Lee, H., & Oh, J.-G. (2010). Integrating climate change policy with a green growth strategy: The case of South Korea. In B. Wakefield (Ed.), *Green tigers: The politics and policy of climate change in northeast Asian democracies* (pp. 14–25). Retrieved from http://www.wilsoncenter.org/sites/default/files/ASIA_090816_Special%20 Report%20144.pd

Leiserowitz, A. (2006). Climate change risk perception and policy preferences: The role of affect, imagery, and values. *Climatic Change, 77,* 45–72.

Loewenstein, G. F., Weber, E. U., Hsee, C. K., & Welch, N. (2001). Risk as feelings. *Psychological Bulletin, 127,* 267–286.

McCright, A. M., & Dunlap, R. E. (2011). The politicization of climate change and polarization in the American public's views of global warming, 2001–2010. *The Sociological Quarterly, 52,* 155–194.

Nisbet, M. C. (2014). Framing, the media and risk communication in policy debates. In H. Cho, T. Reimer, & K. McComas (Eds.), *Sage handbook of risk communication* (pp. 216–227). Newbury Park, CA: Sage.

Pew Research Center. (2010). Pew global attitudes project 2010. Retrieved from http://www.pewglobal.org/2010/05/08/spring-2010-survey-data/

Pew Research Center. (2012). The state of news media: An annual report on American journalism. Retrieved from http://pewresearch.org/pubs/2222/ news-media-network-television-cable-audioo-radio-digital-platforms-local-mobile-devices-tablets-smartphones-native-american-community-newspapers

Priest, S. H. (2001). Misplaced faith: Communication variables as predictor of encouragement for biotechnology development. *Science Communication, 23,* 97–110.

Program on International Policy Attitudes. (2009). World public opinion assessing governments on climate change. Retrieved from http://www.worldpublicopinion.org/pipa/pdf/jul09/WPO_ClimateChange_Jul09_quaire.pdf

Rickard, L. N., Yang, Z. J., Seo, M., & Harrison, T. M. (2014). The "I" in climate: The role of individual responsibility in systematic processing of climate change information. *Global Environmental Change, 26,* 39–52.

Sellström, E., Bremberg, S., Gärling, A., & Hörnquist, J. O. (2000). Risk of childhood injury: Predictors of mothers' perceptions. *Scandinavian Journal of Public Health, 28,* 188–193.

Skitka, L. J. (1999). Ideological and attributional boundaries on public compassion: Reactions to individuals and communities affected by a natural disaster. *Personality and Social Psychology Bulletin, 25,* 793–808.

Slovic, P., Fischhoff, B., & Lichtenstein, S. (1982). Why study risk perception? *Risk Analysis, 2,* 83–93.

Spence, A., Poortinga, W., & Pidgeon, N. (2012). The psychological distance of climate change. *Risk Analysis, 32,* 957–972.

Stone, D. A. (1989). Causal stories and the formation of policy agendas. *Political Science Quarterly, 104,* 281–300.

Taylor, A. L., Dessai, S., & de Bruin, W. B. (2014). Public perception of climate risk and adaptation in the UK: A review of the literature. *Climate Risk Management, 4–5,* 1–16.

The Government of the Republic of Korea. (2003). Second national communication of the Republic of Korea under the United Nations Framework Convention on climate change. Retrieved from http://unfccc.int/resource/docs/natc/kornc02.pdf

Weiner, B. (1993). On sin versus sickness: A theory of perceived responsibility and social motivation. *American Psychologist, 48,* 957–965.

Weiner, B. (1995). *Judgments of responsibility: A foundation for a theory of social conduct.* New York, NY, USA: Guilford Press.

Weinstein, N. D. (1980). Unrealistic optimism about future life events. *Journal of Personality and Social Psychology, 39,* 806–820.

Marketplace Advocacy by the U.S. Fossil Fuel Industries: Issues of Representation and Environmental Discourse

Barbara Miller Gaither and T. Kenn Gaither

School of Communications
Elon University

This study used the circuit of culture to examine advertisements and websites of U.S.-based industry trade groups representing the energy industries of coal (American Coalition for Clean Coal Electricity) and petroleum (American Petroleum Institute). Using a census of all advertisements available through the trade groups' websites during spring 2014, the study identified 4 prominent narratives created by the American Coalition for Clean Coal Electricity and American Petroleum Institute to enhance public support for the industries while fostering uncertainty around climate change and reducing concern for climate initiatives. The research reveals the power inequities surrounding climate discourse by suggesting that wealthy industry trade groups employ a discursive practice of distraction and appropriation of U.S cultural values and mores, essentially shifting public dialogue *from* climate change and potential environmental policies *to* how these policies would hurt the industries and adversely affect the average U.S. citizen.

Opponents have become more sophisticated in mounting resistance to climate campaigns by running equally effective "public will" initiatives and/or manufacturing uncertainty about climate science itself. We've seen this resistance in the carbon industry's multi-million dollar TV ad campaigns for "clean coal." — Cox (2010, p. 125)

Powerful vested interests in the existing carbon-based economy … will continue to
define values and shape self-interest for some time to come" — Brulle and Jenkins
(2006, p. 84)

In June 2013, President Obama released a climate action plan that highlighted the
administration's goal to reduce U.S. greenhouse gas emissions by approximately
17% below 2005 levels by 2020. The action plan—which explicitly stated that
carbon pollution "is the largest driver of climate change" and that carbon
pollution occurs through, among other things, the burning of fossil fuels (coal,
natural gas, and oil)—specifically identified power plants as the largest contri-
butor to carbon emissions in the United States, accounting for approximately
40% of all domestic greenhouse gas pollution. The plan's first item tasked the
Environmental Protection Agency (EPA) with reducing carbon pollution through
carbon standards for both new and existing power plants. Other aspects of the
plan included support for renewable fuels standards, expansion of renewable
energy sources, and the elimination of U.S. fossil fuel tax subsidies in the 2014
budget (Executive Office of the President, 2013, p. 5).

Although the president's action plan leaves little room for debate regarding
the existence of climate change, its potential ramifications, or the fossil fuel
industries' contribution to the problem, a large percentage of the American
public remains unconvinced that climate change is happening and/or is unaware
of the severity of the situation. In 2009, for example, only 44% of the
U.S. population agreed that global warming was a serious problem (Pew
Research Center, 2009). Similarly, in 2010, a Gallup poll found that 53% of
the U.S. population (compared to 73% of the Latin American population)
believed that global warming was a threat to themselves or their families
(Gallup, 2011). As of 2013, a Yale University study found that only 63% of
the U.S. population believed global warming was actually happening (Yale
University, 2010).

Thus, if polling figures are accurate, more than one third of the
U.S. population still harbors doubts regarding climate change and only one
third of citizens believe climate change is caused by human activity, such as
the burning of fossil fuels (Pew Research Center, 2010). According to the Union
of Concerned Scientists, as well as a number of communication scholars (e.g.,
Brulle & Jenkins, 2006; Cox, 2010; Schlichting, 2013), this doubt may stem, in
large part, to strategic communication efforts by the fossil fuel industry. In an
online presentation titled "Exposing the Disinformation Playbook," the Union of
Concerned Scientists explains how the fossil fuel industry has "spread disinformation" to delay action on climate change "in the same way Big Tobacco
mislead the public about the scientific evidence linking smoking to lung cancer
and heart disease" (Union of Concerned Scientists, 2014). Supporting this asser-
tion, between 1990 and 2010, Schlichting (2013) found that a common industry

framing strategy used by the U.S. fossil fuel and electric utility industries was to promote uncertainties regarding climate science, as well as the socioeconomic consequences of regulatory climate policies and treaties that might negatively impact the industries.

Among the chief obstacles to mitigating the worst impacts of climate change, it seems, is a lack of understanding of "the real crisis" (Lakoff, 2010, p. 74), as well as a lack of public support for effective domestic and international policy frameworks (Perkowitz, 2010). As climate change prospects and impacts grow more ominous, Perkowitz (2010) argued that "climate solutions advocates need to take a step back and question their strategies and tactics" (p. 69).

If engendering climate change uncertainty is indeed an objective of the fossil fuel industries, however, also it is fundamentally important to question the strategies that these industries use to connect with the general public. As the United States is the world's second largest emitter of greenhouse gases (World Resources Institute, 2014), U.S. environmental policy has global implications, not just in terms of addressing climate change but also in the U.S.'s amplified voice in the global discussion of climate and sustainability issues.

Thus, this study attempts to shed light on this topic by examining the public discourse used by U.S. fossil fuel industries, specifically coal and petroleum, through the lens of the circuit of culture (du Gay, Hall, Janes, Mackay, & Negus, 1997). The study examines strategic communication by the industry trade groups representing the carbon energy industries of coal (American Coalition for Clean Coal Electricity [ACCCE]) and petroleum (American Petroleum Institute [API]) to enhance public support for the industries while reducing concern and/or support for climate change initiatives.

LITERATURE REVIEW

Marketplace Advocacy

Campaigns by ACCCE and API represent a category of strategic communication known as *marketplace advocacy* (Miller, 2010, 2012; Miller & Sinclair, 2009a; Sinclair & Irani, 2005), a form of corporate issue advocacy designed to encourage public acceptance for a product, service, or industry sector (Arens, Weigold, & Arens, 2008). Although the term *marketplace advocacy* has received limited academic attention, it is commonly used by trade industries (e.g., the American Chemistry Council, the American Forest and Paper Association, and the American Medical Association) to describe strategic communication efforts to confront barriers to the industry and impact public policy. Marketplace advocacy campaigns are sponsored by corporations and industry trade groups in an effort to improve or protect the market for their products, usually by influencing a legislative outcome or a public policy debate (e.g., Cutler & Muehling, 1989; Heath & Nelson, 1986; Nelson, 1994) while maintaining a climate supportive of business activities (Gandy, 1982). Campaign strategies often include deflecting criticism, promoting an organization's image, laying the groundwork for future policy debates, and/or fostering the values of the free enterprise system (Bostdorff & Vibbert, 1994; Cutler & Muehling, 1989; Sethi, 1977). An ultimate goal of marketplace advocacy has been identified as reducing the potential for government intervention in corporate activities (e.g., Cutler & Muehling, 1989; Miller & Sinclair, 2009a, 2009b; Sethi, 1977; Sinclair & Irani, 2005).

Environmental marketplace advocacy campaigns more specifically address current or potential concerns about environmental risks associated with a product or industry (Sinclair & Miller, 2012). Many of these campaigns attempt to downplay an industry's impact on the environment, shifting public attention away from environmental concerns while promoting the benefits of the industry to society. Although environmental marketplace advocacy campaigns may include relatively brief and selective references to corporate activities, most campaigns place a much stronger emphasis on shared values, often distracting attention from serious questions about public issues (Bostdorff & Vibbert, 1994; Miller, 2010). Message strategies praise societal values, condemn oppositional values, and/or associate an organization's products with worthwhile societal goals (Bostdorff & Vibbert, 1994). Environmental marketplace advocacy campaigns have been used by American Electric Power to reduce regulations on coal mining, including strip mining; by Mobil Oil to prevent legislative passage of an excess profits tax directed at oil companies; and by the Chrysler Corporation to slow the implementation of automotive pollution controls (Cutler & Muehling, 1989).

Although some environmental advocates argue that environmental campaigns should focus on articulating progressive environmental values to advance environmental policy (e.g., Crompton, 2008; Lakoff, 2010), marketplace advocacy messages often reassure the public that no radical alterations are necessary and/or emphasize the negative consequences of environmental policies. Environmental organizations must understand how the public responds to these messages to develop effective counter campaigns, particularly given marketplace advocacy's share of voice on environmental issues.

The Circuit of Culture

The application of the circuit of culture model to this study firmly embeds it in the cultural studies area of inquiry. Developed by scholars at the British Centre for Cultural Studies, the circuit had seminal contributions by noted theorists Stuart Hall and Richard Johnson, among others, who grappled with meaning making as a process embedded within and woven throughout cultural practices.

Since its initial application toward the study of the Sony Walkman in the late 1990s, the circuit has been widely used across academic disciplines to analyze a wide range of cultural phenomena.

The five "moments" of the circuit of culture—representation, identity, regulation, consumption, and production—provide nuance that "any analysis of a cultural text or artefact must pass if it is to be adequately studied" (du Gay et al., 1997, p. 3). Because the circuit has no beginning or end, any moment is a possible starting point. The range of possible meanings within the dynamic relationships between and among moments form "articulations," which are, "[any] number of distinct processes whose interaction can and does lead to contingent outcomes" (du Gay et al., 1997, p. 3). Often, those outcomes are temporary but take into account the intricacies of communication, identity, power, meaning, and culture (Curtin & Gaither, 2007, 2012). The cultural economy orientation of the circuit of culture is particularly apropos for an investigation into marketplace advocacy efforts of the ACCCE and API because it provides a framework for viewing these efforts as discursive processes imbued with specific U.S. cultural values, such as individualism, concomitant power inequities, and what it means to be "American" or how America is represented.

The circuit of culture promotes a certain way of seeing and thinking, eschewing a "correct" or "right" way of viewing the process of communication. The model is more concerned with the discursive patterns that inform communication activity through its constitutive moments (Hall, 2013). The application of the circuit of culture provides a way of thinking about marketplace advocacy as a construct that calls into question the communications activities of industry trade groups, suggesting how their work is defined and characterized is a culturally bound process. It could be reductive to debate labels, but this notion suggests that marketplace advocacy challenges some models of persuasive communication and arguably embodies elements of education, public relations, persuasion, information, and propaganda.

The circuit of culture suggests that meaning is partially created through the moment of representation—a situated space where symbols and signs can be arranged to create a particular meaning (Curtin & Gaither, 2007). The circuit of culture can help identify varying, and sometimes conflicting, discourses used to achieve and legitimize organizational objectives by industry trade groups. The model contributes to theory development by dislocating the primacy of economic determinism and factoring in a cultural economic approach, permitting a structured yet flexible method to analyze communication forms that collectively denote marketplace advocacy. Among some of the questions that might constitute the moment of representation include, What is being represented? Is that representation referring to something real or imagined? What is the context, and how does it influence the representation? Applying this orientation toward the advertisements, the moment of representation is only one starting point among the five moments to begin exploring the accrued meanings that constitute marketplace advocacy.

A primary consideration in the moment of representation is how an encoded artifact is decoded through consumption, another moment in the circuit of culture. In advertising, this highlights the link between the producers and consumers, another reminder that all moments of the circuit deserve attention in the process of meaning creation:

> Objects like the Walkman ... do not possess their own instrinsic meaning, and they cannot express their meaning for us. Advertising is the cultural language, which speaks *on behalf of* the product. Advertising makes commodities speak. It must *address the buyer*. It must create an identification between the customer and the product. ... No matter how much we like and admire the people in the advertisements, if we cannot see or imagine ourselves in that role, we will often be more reluctant to shell out the money required to purchase the commodity (du Gay et al., 1997, p. 25).

Representation suggests advertisements circumscribe meanings, essentially nullifying some meanings and privileging others. As Leve (2012) noted, "The process of creating and trying to fix a particular message or meaning to representations is integral to the work of those whose job it is to build and maintain the value of a commodity" (p. 6). Here, "idea" could be substituted for commodity as currency in meaning making, leading to how power structures such as big business attempt to monopolize meanings through strategic communication and the process of representation.

Although many marketplace advocacy campaigns narrowly target specific publics through lobbying efforts, many campaigns also target nonexpert lay audiences. Campaign strategies often involve event sponsorship, "grassroots" public relations, mass media advertising, and media relations in national news outlets (Miller, 2012; Sinclair & Miller, 2012). An overarching goal of this research is to shed some initial light on the means by which the fossil fuel industries legitimize certain environmental narratives in the United States by encoding selected materials, especially those targeting mass audiences, with strategic messages. In the parlance of the circuit of culture, these materials are sites of contested meaning. The discursive patterns embedded in and surrounding these materials are a response to an issue or concern. In this way, they represent what Hall (2013) called a "process of translation," where the persistence of difference and power is immutable (p. 45).

Focusing the circuit of culture lens on campaigns by ACCCE and API amplifies the relationship between campaign producers, or strategic communicators, and the range of meanings encoded in the various texts that constitute their respective campaigns, leading to these research questions:

RQ1: What meanings are constructed in discourse by trade groups for the fossil fuel industries for coal (ACCCE) and petroleum (API) for American audiences?

RQ2: What norms do these discourses legitimize regarding the industries and the environment?

METHOD

We used a qualitative content analysis of all advertisements available through the trade groups' websites during February and March 2014. As this study involved a census rather than a sample of all of the trade groups' advertisements (dating back to 2012 for API and 2011 for ACCCE), this period fully captured the trade groups' advertising throughout recent years. The unit of analysis was each advertisement. For API, 101 advertisements were analyzed—47 television, 11 radio, seven online, and 36 print ads. All of the advertisements for API were available under the News and Media tab of its website, which featured ads for numerous campaigns (e.g., Energy Tomorrow, Energy Citizens, EnergyFromShale.org, etc.). For ACCCE, 17 advertisements were analyzed —14 television and three print ads. All of the advertisements for ACCCE were available under Ad Archive of the Press Room tab, which redirected viewers to its America's Power campaign. The API website (www.api.org) and ACCCE website (www.cleancoalusa.org) then were used to contextualize advertising references and for sponsor identification, especially considering API's use of various campaign sponsor identities (as discussed in the Findings section).

Although all moments of the circuit of culture inform the study, given the research questions, this study focused primarily on representation. This method views the studied advertisements as texts, or representations, composed of symbols and signs. The producers of these materials occupy an intermediary position by reappropriating cultural symbols for strategic purposes to curry support with the general public. As such, the producers are cultural intermediaries who encode dominant meanings within their communications based on their strategic goals, through representations they believe will enhance consumption of their messages. Although the ACCCE and API certainly have specific objectives unique to their respective industries, the purpose of this study is to broadly examine the strategies used by the fossil fuel industries to legitimize certain narratives and, in turn, write others out of consideration. In the context of this investigation, an underlying supposition was made that among the strategic goals of the ACCCE and API are to: (a) generate public support for the industry, thereby reducing public opposition to the industry (Miller, 2012); (b) prevent and/or eliminate environmental regulations that negatively impact the industries (Schlichting, 2013; Sinclair & Miller, 2012); and (c) engender uncertainty regarding climate change science and relevant climate policies (Schlichting, 2013; Sinclair & Miller, 2012; Union of Concerned Scientists, 2014).

Data Analysis and Interpretation

The "moments" offer sites of analysis and direction to deconstruct a "text" such as an advertisement with some explicit assumptions. First, the circuit of culture provides a structured approach to possible readings of a text; there are multiple meanings, so the efficacy of inquiry rests on qualitative content analysis with detailed description to unveil narratives. Second, meaning, as explicated here, is fluid and unfixed. The dynamic nature of the circuit of culture and its interrelationships among moments symbolizes the decentering of one fixed meaning. Finally, because a comprehensive adoption of the circuit would require equal weight given to all moments, this study considers all moments but focuses primarily on representation—"the practice of constructing meaning through signs and language" (du Gay et al., 1997, p. 24). Because the study draws heavily on the symbiosis of American symbols, culture, and meaning making, the moment of identity was given secondary consideration. As Hall (2013) offered, "it is difficult to know what being 'English' or indeed, French, German, South African or Japanese *means* outside all the ways in which our ideas of national identity or national cultures have been represented" (p. xxi). Hall's reasoning augments the link between representation and identity without lessening any other moments in the circuit of culture, an approach this study mirrors.

In viewing the ads as texts, we analyzed the subtexts of each ad relative to the manifest content, guided by the circuit of culture (du Gay et al., 1997; Hall, 2013), to identify and highlight discourses encoded in the advertisements. All aspects of the advertisements were examined by the researchers, including visuals, text, and/or audio, through a process of emergent coding and categorized as types of representations, one of the five "moments" within the circuit. This included coding text, language, and images from the advertisements that exemplified categories, then modifying and refining categories on the basis of subsequent readings of the advertisements. Instances that did not fit with the initial categories were used to adapt, expand, and refocus the guiding theoretical frameworks of the study. These systematic and original categories of analysis were identified based on "recurring regularities" in the content (Patton, 1990, p. 403) until no new categories emerged from the data, suggesting that information saturation was achieved (Wimmer & Dominick, 2014). Examples from the texts are used throughout the analysis to document categories of representations.

FINDINGS

The analysis revealed four prominent narratives in the analyzed materials of ACCCE and API: (a) the industry supporter: America's everyman/everywoman; (b) the "other:" the president, the EPA, politicians, and the uninformed/unenlightened; (c) the industry as paternal caretaker for American citizens; and (d) industry supporters as the moral majority. Each is explicated in turn in this section, which includes numerous partial quotations from corresponding trade groups' websites.

The Industry Supporter: America's Everyman/Everywoman

Virtually all of the industry ads studied attempted to represent an industry supporter as an "everyman" and/or "everywoman." Ads emphasized that potential environmental regulations impacted not just coal and petroleum industry workers but all U.S. citizens. Featuring individuals of all ethnicities/races, gender, ages, and occupations, a subtext seemed to be that the tentacles of these industries reach well beyond those working at refineries, on wells, and/or underground. Individuals featured in television ads ranged from firemen and family farmers promoting the development of natural gas, to a nurse and a businessman being bucked off a bull in a "rodeo" ad in support of the coal industry, to a mom of two children reading economic headlines on her iPad discussing her opposition to "raising energy taxes." By portraying diversity in multiple facets, the ads suggest the essence of the industries is the essence of America.

In fact, API created a range of campaigns targeting individuals based on a variety of concerns, identities, and issues. For example, the Energy Nation campaign "brings together the hard-working people of America's oil and natural gas industry to ensure our voices are heard by our nation's policymakers." Meanwhile, the Energy Citizens campaign targets those who work outside the industry and is used to encourage citizens to take action on energy policies. The America's Choice campaign, which seems similar to Energy Citizens in its objectives, is even more direct in its efforts to encourage political action, calling on Republicans, Democrats, and Independents to get involved in "choosing to produce and refine more American energy." Campaign rhetoric calls on individuals to "join together to re-energize America" by supporting domestic energy production, emphasizing that "we're the global leader in natural gas production and *can* be a leader in oil."

In a series of print ads from API's Choose Energy campaign, "I choose energy" is written in script font to portray cursive handwriting, suggesting a personalized message. The ads feature a young Caucasian father; a male Caucasian plant worker; and a young, smartly dressed African-American woman. A series of other ads opposing a potentially higher ethanol mandate include an Asian woman at the grocery store shocked by her bill, an African-American man appearing sad as he pays an auto mechanic for work on his car, and a distressed Caucasian woman in a business suit stranded on the highway. The text in the latter ad states, "Your engine won't like it [the ethanol mandate], but your mechanic will." Similarly, the Vote4Energy campaign uses first names and individuals talking about why they're "an energy voter." Each commercial highlights one individual talking about why the viewer should care about energy policy. The ads feature "Kim" (a middle-aged Caucasian woman in a business suit), "Jason" (a young, hip African-American man), "Edward" (a middle-aged man with a dark complexion in a sweater vest), "Felice" (an African-American woman with small baby), "Aaron" (a young Caucasian man with satchel across his shoulder, who appears to be a student), "Kelsie" (a young Caucasian woman who also appears to be a student), and "Dan" (an older, slightly balding Caucasian man, dressed in a vest and loafers).

Perhaps the most prominent of the API campaigns is "Energy Tomorrow." Ads in this series appear frequently in mainstream television, particularly during morning and primetime news shows; these ads were also aired repeatedly throughout the winter 2014 Olympics on NBC. Although an attractive blonde woman in a business suit acts as the spokeswoman, the ads consistently feature people in all types of business/work attire standing behind the spokeswoman at the ad's opening or close. The tagline reads, "The *people* [emphasis in original] of America's oil and natural gas industry," suggesting that the ad has been signed by a diverse group of people, all with interests in oil and natural gas.

Both ACCCE and API portray the industries as fundamentally American, generating a dominant discourse predicated on an imaginary public embracing a particular viewpoint. Advertisements emphasize families and communities with images of the heartland and Americana, tapping into cultural constructs of what it means to be American or what constitutes Americanness. The employment of perfect cultural symbols constitutes a simulacrum of America that is too utopian and dismissive of challenging discourses to be wholly real. In one ad for API, a man and woman walk hand in hand with a small child down a dusty road toward farmland while the narrator explains, "The future of this land is in our hands." Visuals in print and television ads include a baby in a red wagon, basketball and baseball games, cheerleaders, and American flags waving on front porches and in the distance. Names and locations of individuals and businesses are used to personalize the industries. Stotts Drug Store, for example, is featured in an API ad that explains, "Across America, people are joining together in places like Searcy, Arkansas, to make their towns prosper. The oil and natural gas industry is part of these communities." Similarly, individuals at the Thunder Basin Coal Company are featured in an ad by ACCCE. The language in these ads (i.e., audio and text) emphasizes "communities" (e.g., "In communities across the country, we're creating jobs ...") and inclusivity (e.g., "*let's* build" and "it's *our* choice").

In addition, the ads are replete with images of America and patriotic themes. The narrator in one ACCCE ad highlights the fact that coal is "America's home field advantage," by showing onscreen images of baseball fields, American flags, and Open for Business signs. Similarly, in an API Energy Tomorrow ad titled "Investing in America's Future," visuals of America (either the flag or in text) appear six times in 30 seconds. Likewise, in a Vote4Energy radio ad ("It's Time for Energy"), "America" or "American(s)" are mentioned seven times in 30 seconds. Both API and ACCCE emphasize the need to produce more oil, natural gas, or coal "*right here at home.*"

The "Other:" The President, the EPA, Politicians, and the Uninformed/ Unenlightened

Hall (2013) asked, "Why is 'otherness' so compelling an object of representation?" (p. 224). This question subsumes the fundamental issues of power inscribed in the circuit of culture, drawing attention toward the "other" as part of power. As Derrida (1972) theorized, there is always a power relation between oppositions. Part of what something is, then, is through what it is not, making the "other" essential to meaning (Hall, 2013). Advertisements for both API and ACCCE create an image of the "other," or those that would oppose the industry. The most prominent "other" in both API and ACCCE ads is the president, the EPA, and/or Washington politicians. In API ads, for example, the narrator calls on viewers to "tell the president to fix the mandate for higher ethanol," suggesting the mandate is broken and needs to be fixed. Ads supporting the Keystone XL Pipeline similarly tell audiences to "tell President Obama we need it [the pipeline] now" and emphasize that "it's up to him."

API is selective in its use of an "other" discourse, limiting direct references to the president and the EPA to campaigns that oppose specific environmental initiatives (e.g., the higher ethanol mandate for cars and construction of the Keystone XL Pipeline). In campaign ads showcasing the identity of the industry supporter (i.e., America's Everyman/Everywoman)—such as Energy Citizens, Energy Tomorrow, and Vote4Energy—an "other" identity is avoided. When the president, the administration, the EPA, and/or "Washington politicians" are mentioned, however, the ads conclude with taglines such as "FillUpOnFacts. org" or close simply by saying that the ad was "paid for by the American Petroleum Institute" (using only the trade group's identity without referencing one of the group's many campaigns).

Similarly, ACCCE ads frequently refer to "Obama and *his* [emphasis added] EPA" and "politicians in Washington and *their* [emphasis added] policies." These ads demonstrate a strong antagonism between the "everyman" and the "other" as evidenced by an ad featuring a boxing ring in which a diverse group of individuals have been knocked out. Another ACCCE ad features a rodeo in which individuals ranging from a man in a business suit to a woman in scrubs with a stethoscope attempt to ride a bull. Just as the audio refers to "the administration" and "EPA regulations," a rodeo clown is seen laughing menacingly as the woman gets bucked off the bull.

Images of physical violence in sport from boxing to rodeo delineate power imbalance by positioning the federal government as a formidable foe against the powerless "everyman." Moreover, the physical spaces of a boxing ring and rodeo circle metaphorically represent contested spaces in the production of meaning with power operating on several levels. The everyman is constricted and physically defeated. In turn, producers strive to frame a dominant discourse that is

53

decidedly pro-industry by representing power strictures as bullies. This stance relates to the moment of regulation by illustrating the policies enacted by Washington as a metonym for the federal government exerting its legislative powers.

Many of the ads also suggest the "other" is, in fact, either unintelligent and/or uninformed to support proposed EPA regulations and/or environmental policies. Campaign ads concluding with "FillUpOnFacts.org" suggest people would *obviously* support the industry if they only knew the facts. In one API ad, a woman who allowed fracking on her land explains, "We talked with experts and learned the facts. And guess what? It's safe." Ads supporting construction of the Keystone XL Pipeline, meanwhile, emphasize the pipeline should be built "after 4 years of federal review." Again, the subtext for audiences is that the issue has been overstudied and an ill-defined "we" (i.e., American viewers) would be foolish not to proceed with construction. Other API ads similarly tell audiences, "Don't be fooled" in reference to proposed energy tax changes. Pro-industry policies are referred to as "forward-thinking"; conversely, proposed EPA regulations are deemed "heavy-handed." One ACCCE ad explains, "It's energy economics 101. ... By failing to understand the importance of affordable power, the EPA is failing America."

In addition to the U.S. president, the EPA, politicians, and the uninformed, a final discourse of the "other" includes the unenlightened. In one of its more antagonistic campaigns, API has a series of cartoon print ads titled "Life without Fossil Fuels." In one ad titled "It's Cold Outside," people carrying various signs of protest (all of which begin with "NO ...") stand in the snow outside an individual's home while a man sits inside wearing short sleeves and reading the newspaper. A drink with an umbrella sits beside him on a table. The protesters, who wear heavy coats, scarfs, and earmuffs, appear to be freezing cold as one protestor knocks on the window and asks, "Can we come in? We're tired of being out in the cold!" Another ad features a cartoon version of Uncle Sam, another metonym for the U.S. government, sitting on what appear to be barrels of oil; he is tied up in various ways, unable to access the oil.

Similarly, in ACCCE ads, the unenlightened "other" is also portrayed subtly as those who would support environmental regulations, particularly those policies that would hinder the coal industry. In an ad titled "Rock of our Prosperity," the narrator explains how "Washington has taken us down ... a path relying on fads, not fuels, a path leading away from energy independence." As the narrator references "fads," the camera pans to a scene of a street protest in which picketers wear green hats. The image of the protesters in green is then juxtaposed with a vast coal pile hundreds of feet high. The implication for viewers is that "green" is a passing "fad," one lacking the substance and viability of a path relying on the abundant fuel of coal.

The Industry: Paternal Caretaker for American Citizens

In addition to the supporter and "other" discourses, this study found that ACCCE and API campaigns have also created a dominant narrative for the industries as a paternal caretaker for U.S. citizens. An underlying message embedded throughout their advertising is that the industries represent the average citizen. In reference to support for domestic energy production, one API ad authoritatively explains, "We need it, now more than ever."

To communicate this message, many of the ads rely on fear appeals with the supposition that "if we don't [support the industry], we're all in trouble." In API ads, the administration's proposed elimination of energy industry subsidies is reframed as "new energy taxes," and individuals explain how "a tax on the oil and natural gas industry … is really a tax on us." A variety of individuals explain how the policies will "definitely kill some jobs," "harm the country," and are a "big mistake." In one ad, a young woman at a table explains to viewers, "Washington says they're billing the companies, but they're really billing me." Meanwhile, an African-American man in a bow tie plainly states, "It is not a tax on the oil and gas industry, it is a tax on families." Another ad on the same issue concludes, "We're gonna get hit from all directions." The repetition of Washington as synecdoche for the U.S. government essentially creates a divisiveness that fits into a discourse of othering.

The ACCCE uses a similar fear-based appeal to represent the industry as caregiver to the average U.S. citizen. In an ad opposing new EPA mercury regulations on power plants, a senior public affairs manager for a Colorado-based power plant paints a dire outlook if regulations are not stopped:

> It's not just raising the costs to individuals at their homes, it's about what it does to manufacturers, what it does to agriculture industry. In the end, we run the risk of being uncompetitive. Businesses could move out of this town, they could move out of this state, they could move out of this country.

Likewise, in another ACCCE ad titled "Fairness," the narrator explains,

> We're hearing a lot about fairness from this administration. But is it fair for their EPA to increase what Americans pay for electricity, by imposing new expensive regulations on coal? With all the pain at the pump, now is the time to act before those who can least afford it, feel even greater pain at the plug.

Many of the ads juxtapose images of desolation, abandoned buildings, broken glass, For Sale signs, and sad young children, all subdued by dark tones, with a fossil fuel industry–based future that is bright and promising. These images are particularly stark because they conflict with the simulacrum of Americana that is encoded in other representations. When discussing the possibilities of either petroleum (API ads) or coal (ACCCE ads), the imagery shifts to include family farms, the American flag waving outside homes in fields, young children saying the Pledge of Allegiance in school, a young couple standing beside a beautiful stream, and young children playing baseball. Likewise, background music shifts from dark and menacing to uplifting as the narrator speaks with a more promising tone of voice. "Closed" signs are now "Open for Business."

Industry Supporters as the Moral Majority

Finally, campaigns by both ACCCE and API discursively represent the industry supporter as being part of a moral majority of U.S. citizens. Support for the industry, be it coal or petroleum, is encoded as the only moral choice, referred to simply as "a good thing." Pro-industry policies are portrayed as pro-job and pro-American; anything else (i.e., proposed EPA regulations and environmental policies) equals a lack of support for fellow Americans.

In an API Vote4Energy ad, for example, Jason, a young, smartly dressed African-American man, states simply, "Developing our own resources right here. It's the *right* thing to do." In the same ad, Jason explains, "Nothing is more important than getting people back to work. Nothing." In another Vote4Energy ad, Kelsie, a young Caucasian woman dressed in jeans, explains, "Developing more energy here is vital to turning this economy around. We've gotta do it." According to API ads, domestic energy production is "good for our kids" and "good for everyone." Meanwhile, "developing Canadian oil sands for U.S. consumers ... could put a million more Americans to work."

ACCCE advertisements convey a similar message that support for the coal industry is the correct moral decision. In one television ad, Cheryl, an Arch Coal Company production trainer, describes in a sympathetic fashion, hand over her heart, how "many people have lost their jobs in a poor, sluggish economy." Other ads describe how "today, too many Americans are just trying to hang on to their jobs" and subsequently highlight how coal "helps create jobs" and "keep(s) energy costs in check" and "jobs in America." The shift to economic empowerment relies on cultural mores embroidered into American culture for producers to formulate a persuasive moral argument. In doing so, producers privilege the economic over the environmental, suggesting the "true" America is awash in economic empowerment and opportunity while dearticulating any environmental considerations.

DISCUSSION

To shed light on the ways in which the coal and petroleum industries in the United States encode materials in an attempt to generate favorable public attitudes toward the industries while reducing support for climate change initiatives, this study jointly examined the public discourse used by the trade groups representing these industries. Although aspects of the ACCCE and API advertising were certainly unique to the respective industries (e.g., API's use of multiple campaigns), four overarching narratives of representation emerged throughout strategic communication used by both groups: the industry supporter (America's everyman/everywoman), the "other" (the president, the EPA, politicians, and the uninformed/unenlightened), the industry (as paternal caretaker for American citizens), and the industry supporter (as reflective of the country's moral majority).

The four narratives revealed in the research are constructed in and through discourse. As such, these narratives represent discursive practices that are dynamic and polysemic. To borrow from Laclau (1990), every identity is *dislocated* because it relies on an "other" to both deny and reify its identity. This study locates the moment of identity in these sites of dislocation: The everyman is not the everywoman, and vice versa, but both are part of America. In turn, America is strategically reconstructed by the fossil fuels industries to appeal to Americans. This reconstruction of Americana relates to the moment of representation, which illuminates the conjoining of representation and identity. This relationship suggests not only a notion of what America is but also what it *isn't*. Moreover, it suggests that "America" is more than a simple binary construct by alluding to an "authentic" America representation.

Similarly, the industry supporter represented as the moral majority constitutes power as projected by a constructed "moral majority" and in response to that majority. In both cases, the "other" serves a critical function in meaning making. How that meaning is created and to what ends are indicative of marketplace advocacy campaigns used by businesses and industry trade groups to impact public policy, especially to reduce or prevent environmental legislation that would negatively impact an industry sector.

In this way, the representations are responsive to external forces and dependent upon them to generate meanings and influence public opinion. This study's findings that the fossil fuel industries in the United States legitimize discourses by employing strategic exclusion toward complex ends; these industries simultaneously create a dominant discourse and cloud opposing narratives, or wholly reject them. In essence, this approach is purposely ambiguous, as is the bricolage of front groups and agencies API uses to connect with audiences (e.g., Energy Tomorrow, Vote4Energy, Energy Citizens, etc.) that ostensibly introduce doubt as a tool of obfuscation in public discourse.

This article does not suggest that such industry groups are responsible for the large percentage of the American public that remains unconvinced that climate change is happening and underestimates the severity of the situation. It does, however, illustrate the relative power of such groups in launching a fusillade of campaigns and spending millions of dollars to oppose energy policies, perhaps some of which use the questioning of the science behind climate change as motivation. Moreover, the research revealed the complexity of industry communications campaigns and sophisticated use of language and symbols to reinforce strategic positions. The challenge for environmental organizations is to develop equally as persuasive counter campaigns, often with limited economic means, to provide formidable alternative viewpoints in a public dialogue rife with uncertainty.

A de facto residual of this uncertainty is a general marketplace advocacy position that change is not needed and to serve as a distraction from other salient issues. Through the ACCCE and API's "Industry Supporter" representation, the campaigns feature patchwork initiatives tailored to a broad range of audiences. The range of target publics and tailored messages centers around a common representation of "America" and what it means to be American. Notably, selected exclusion of messaging such as environmental degradation is contrasted with inclusive language (e.g., "*let's* build" and "*our* choice") as a dialectical device. In "the other" identity, the narrative of the "other" subverts power of authority by suggesting "we" can affect change. This identity recalibrates power differentials by placing the public sphere in the same sphere as politicians, which represents a perception of agency to the individual. The research supports the position by many scientists and environmental scholars that among the goals of the fossil fuel industries are to limit and/or defeat relevant U.S. climate change policies, including establishing EPA regulations for carbon and mercury emissions, reducing energy subsidies, opposing an ethanol mandate, and permitting for coal-fired power plants.

Although Hall (2013) suggested that no moment in the circuit of culture circumscribes another, he did draw links between representation and identity in a discussion of symbolic practices that bind communities by creating shared identities (p. xxi). Similarly, this study illuminates—but does not privilege—the link between the moments of representation and identity, which considers the segmentation of publics, who cannot be ignored as consumers of advertising messages. As demonstrated by this research, both ACCCE and API use a broad cross section of individuals in their advertisements. This impressive broadness factored in race/ethnicity, gender, age, and other demographics. In doing so, these industry groups suggest that the issues they promulgate are of importance to *all* Americans. What it means to be an American is reproduced by industry groups that formulate a vision of what "we" need to do against "them," pitting patriotism and morality against the construct of environmental and other opposition groups and politicians. Tapping into patriotism links a polemic to that which is held sacred, wrapped in cultural reverence for nationalism, country, and pride. This articulation of American values is so utopian in nature that it obviates a "true" America, instead injecting emotional appeals into cultural references to project an idealized version of America.

CONCLUSION

This study augments previous studies using the circuit of culture by casting strategic communicators as cultural intermediaries who encode campaign materials to create representations. In the case of this study of environmental marketplace advocacy, however, those representations are not wholly constructive, nor are they necessarily mutually beneficial. In addition to fostering uncertainty around climate change, the research illustrates that U.S. fossil fuel industries are really shifting the public dialogue *from* climate change and how environmental policies might help to mitigate it *to* how these policies would hurt the industries, resulting in a loss of jobs and affecting the average U.S. citizen. Building on this notion, the four prominent narratives in this study center around two themes: One is distraction, or a purposeful attempt to shift attention from issues of science and the environment to a politic of economy and self-determination; the second is a reappropriation of American cultural values and mores to shape a perceived "correct" way of thinking. In this way, there is a moral center in which baseball, the American flag, and the Pledge of Allegiance are among the key tools of persuasion. The distinctly American influence suggests that what constitutes "marketplace advocacy" in the United States and the tools of persuasion under its banner are not generalizable to other cultures without further research.

Additional research could consider specific political outcomes of marketplace advocacy campaigns, as well as actual strategies and tactics used to influence approval for the advocated industry. API's Energy Tomorrow campaign, for example, encourages citizens to take action against policies such as EPA regulations on greenhouse gas emissions by joining the Energy Citizens movement, e-mailing Congress, and sharing information with others. Additional online and social media efforts of ACCCE include a YouTube channel ("America's Power") and a Behind the Plug blog, which presents energy news and legislative updates. Case study investigation into these tactics relative to specific public policies may shed further light on direct political outcomes of these types of marketplace advocacy efforts.

A limitation of this research is the scope of analyzed content. It focused on mainstream advertising only, which represents only one swath of the communications arsenal of industry trade groups. Also, there is a degree of subjectivity from the analysis, although the circuit of culture provided a structure for studying the advertisements that permitted an investigation into meanings and identities created by these campaigns for audiences. Further research might more fully factor in the other moments of the circuit, pulling into the fray issues of ethics, the regulatory environment surrounding marketplace advocacy (e.g., regulations on corporate spending in elections), and the effectiveness of industry representations through consumption from media effects research, among other possibilities. Research of this nature is fundamental to understanding the strategies that these industries use to connect with the general public while reducing support for climate change initiatives (Schlichting, 2013; Union of Concerned Scientists, 2014).

Although other strategies beyond those identified here may have been unique to either the ACCCE or the API campaigns, these findings suggest a strong commonality in the trade groups' representation. Especially when considered in concert with other research on the role of marketplace advocacy campaigns—including their ability to build and shape public agendas regarding the coal industry (Miller, 2010) and to connect with audiences via values-based messaging (Sinclair & Miller, 2012)—the findings of this study are potentially quite significant for environmental advocates. Scientific "truth" and empirical research often become hidden behind layers of competing discourses, and few citizens are likely to carefully scrutinize the messages they receive from industry trade groups. Marketplace advocacy of this nature, supported through deep pockets capable of frequent messaging, becomes a powerful voice in public discourse on industry, science, and the environment.

REFERENCES

Arens, C., Weigold, M. F., & Arens, W. F. (2008). *Contemporary advertising* (11th ed.). Boston, MA: McGraw-Hill

Bostdorff, D. M., & Vibbert, S. L. (1994). Values advocacy: Enhancing organizational images, deflecting public criticism, and grounding future arguments. *Public Relations Review, 20*(2), 141–158. doi:10.1016/0363-8111(94)90055-8

Brulle, R. J., & Jenkins, J. C. (2006). Spinning our way to sustainability? *Organization & Environment, 19*, 82–87. doi:10.1177/1086026605285587

Cox, J. R. (2010). Beyond frames: Recovering the strategic in climate communication. *Environmental Communication, 4*, 122–133. doi: 10.1080/17524030903516555

Crompton, T. (2008). *Weathercocks and signposts: The environment movement at a crossroads.* Retrieved from http://assets.wwf.org.uk/downloads/weathercocks_report2.pdf

Curtin, P., & Gaither, T. K. (2007). *International public relations: Negotiating culture, identity, and power.* Thousand Oaks, CA: Sage.

Curtin, P., & Gaither, T. (2012). *Globalization and public relations in postcolonial nations: Challenges and opportunities.* Amherst, NY: Cambria Press.

Cutler, B. D., & Muehling, D. D. (1989). Advocacy advertising and the boundaries of commercial speech. *Journal of Advertising, 18*(3), 40–50. doi:10.1080/00913367.1989.10673160

Derrida, J. (1972). *Positions.* Chicago, IL: University of Chicago Press.

Executive Office of the President. (2013). *The President's Climate Action Plan.* Retrieved July 7, 2016, from http://www.whitehouse.gov/sites/default/files/image/president27sclimateactionplan.pdf

Gallup. (2011). *Fewer Americans, Europeans view global warming as a threat.* Retrieved from http://www.gallup.com/poll/147203/Fewer-Americans-Europeans-View-Global-Warming-As-Threat.aspx

Gandy, O. H. (1982). Public relations and public policy: The structuration of dominance in the information age. In E. L. Toth & R. L. Heath (Eds.), *Rhetorical and critical approaches to public relations* (pp. 131–163). Hillsdale, NJ: Erlbaum.

Hall, S. (2013). The spectacle of the other. In S. Hall, J. Evans, & S. Nixon (Eds.), *Representation* (2nd ed., pp. 215–271). London, UK· Sage.

Heath, R. L., & Nelson, R. A. (1986). *Issues management: Corporate policy making in an information society*. Beverly Hills, CA: Sage.

Laclau, E. (1990). *New reflections on the revolution of our time*. London, UK: Verso.

Lakoff, G. (2010). Why it matters how we frame the environment. *Environmental Communication, 4* (1), 70–81. doi:10.1080/17524030903529749

Leiserowitz, A., Smith, N. & Marlon, J.R. (2010) *Americans' Knowledge of Climate Change*. Yale University. New Haven, CT: Yale Project on Climate Change Communication.

Leve, A. (2012, December). *The circuit of culture as a generative tool of contemporary analysis: Examining the constructon of an education commodity*. Paper presented at the Joint Australian Association for Research in Education and Asia-Pacific Educational Research Association Conference (AARE-APERA 2012) World Education Research Association (WERA) Focal Meeting, Sydney, Australia.

Miller, B. M. (2010). Community stakeholders and marketplace advocacy: A model of advocacy, agenda building, and industry approval. *Journal of Public Relations Research, 22*(1), 85–112. doi:10.1080/10627260903170993

Miller, B. M. (2012). *Marketplace advocacy campaigns: Generating public support for business and industry*. Amherst, NY: Cambria Press.

Miller, B. M., & Sinclair, J. (2009a). Community stakeholder responses to advocacy advertising: Trust, accountability, and the persuasion knowledge model. *Journal of Advertising, 38*(2), 37–52. doi:10.2753/JOA0091-3367380203

Miller, B. M., & Sinclair, J. (2009b). A model of public response to marketplace advocacy. *Journalism & Mass Communication Quarterly, 86*(3), 613–630. doi:10.1177/107769900908600310

Nelson, R. A. (1994). Issues communication and advocacy: Contemporary and ethical challenges. *Public Relations Review, 20*(3), 225–231.

Patton, M. (1990). *Qualitative evaluation and research methods*. Beverly Hills, CA: Sage.

Perkowitz, R. M. (2010). Climate communications: Conflicts and opportunities. *Environmental Communication, 4*(1), 66–69. doi:10.1080/17524030903516514

Pew Research Center. (2009). *Global warming seen as a major problem around the world less concern in the U.S., China and Russia*. Retrieved from http://www.pewglobal.org/2009/12/02/global-warming-seen-as-a-major-problem-around-the-world-less-concern-in-the-us-china-and-russia/

Pew Research Center. (2010). *Little change in opinions about global warming*. Retrieved from http://www.people-press.org/2010/10/27/little-change-in-opinions-about-global-warming/

Schlichting, I. (2013). Strategic framing of climate change by industry actors: A meta-analysis. *Environmental Communication, 7*(4), 493–511. doi:10.1080/17524032.2013.812974

Sethi, S. P. (1977). *Advocacy advertising and large corporations*. Lexington, MA: Lexington Books.

Sinclair, J., & Irani, T. (2005). Advocacy advertising for biotechnology: The effect of public accountability on corporate trust and attitude toward the ad. *Journal of Advertising, 34*(3), 59–73. doi:10.1080/00913367.2005.10639203

Sinclair, J., & Miller, B. M. (2012). Public response before and after a crisis: Appeals to values and outcomes for environmental attitudes. In L. Ahern & D. Bortree (Eds.), *Talking green: Exploring contemporary issues in environmental communications* (pp. 107–130). New York, NY: Peter Lang.

Union of Concerned Scientists. (2014). *Exposing the disinformation playbook: An interactive slide show*. Retrieved from http://www.ucsusa.org/global_warming/solutions/fight-misinformation/global-warming-facts-and-fossil-fuel-industry-disinformation-tactics.html

Wimmer, R. D., & Dominick, J. R. (2014). *Mass media research: An introduction* (10th ed.). Boston, MA: Cengage Learning.

World Resources Institute. (2014). *6 graphs explain the world's top 10 emitters*. Retrieved from http://www.wri.org/blog/2014/11/6-graphs-explain-world%E2%80%99s-top-10-emitters

Digital Media, Cycle of Contention, and Sustainability of Environmental Activism: The Case of Anti-PX Protests in China

Jun Liu

Department of Media, Cognition and Communication
Centre for Communication and Computing
University of Copenhagen

Although scholars have studied issues arising from digital activism, most have failed to scrutinize the possible interconnections that might be found within digitally mediated political contention. To advance such an understanding, this study employs the concept of "cycles of contention" to investigate recurrent mechanisms of protest in contemporary society. This study takes as its case 7 anti-petrochemical (anti-PX) protests in China from 2007 to 2014, during which 54 in-depth interviews were conducted. Whereas traditional media coverage legitimizes and modularizes anti-PX protests, facilitates the adoption of digital media as part of the repertoire of contention, and sustains political contention in the long run, the use of digital media enables protestors to diffuse contention widely and quickly and allows them to learn from the experiences of the past. This study concludes that the sustainability of digitally mediated environmental activism is shaped by the specific communication ecology in China.

"... Pollution: Xiamen residents do not want it! Kunming residents do not want it! Shifang residents do not want it! ... We Maoming residents do not want it either!"
  - Message A

"A PX project that has been forbidden in Xiamen and discarded by Dalian will be extended in Zhenhai, Ningbo ... PX is paraxylene, which easily leads to cancer and pathological changes of the reproductive system; please forward this message if you live in Ningbo!"
 - Message B[1]

At the end of March 2014, a message (Message A) went viral through both the internet and mobile phones in China, including text messaging, online forums, the online instant messenger QQ, the Chinese microblogging platform *weibo*, and Wechat, a Whatsapp-style social networking app. Following the dispersion of the message, thousands of residents of Maoming in Guangdong Province took to the streets, holding signs protesting a proposed petrochemical (PX) project. On-the-spot images and videos of protests, together with environmental and health concerns over the project, proliferated on the internet and mobile social networks, attracting widespread news coverage in both national and international media (e.g., BBC, 2014).

The anti-PX protest in Maoming is more than just one of the thousands of political contentions in contemporary China that has caught public attention and manifested the increasing adoption of information and communication technologies (ICTs) as means of protest. Instead, it is also the latest in—and a reminder of—a series of protests against PX projects in China between 2007 and 2014, following the activism in Xiamen (Xie & Zhao, 2007), Kunming (Chang, 2013), and Shifang (FlorCruz, 2012), as the message exemplifies. Similar to the protest in Maoming, the wide and rapid diffusion of Message B via the internet and mobile phones launched a 4-day protest with more than 5,000 participants against a PX project in Ningbo, Zhejiang province, in 2012 (Liu & Yan, 2012). Besides a call for further distribution, the message articulated that the protests recalled the ones in Xiamen and Dalian. In short, earlier anti-PX protests spawn subsequent ones, underpinning a movement continuity against the PX project in China.

How can we explain these protests—especially explain the continuity between these digitally mediated anti-PX protests? Which factors lead to the continuity of the adoption of digital media for political activism here? A number of thorough studies have documented the increasingly prominent role of digital media in political activism in the processes of claims making, network bridging, information distribution, resource accumulation, repertoire diversification, and movement mobilization, to mention a few (e.g., Castells, 2012; Earl & Kimport, 2011; van de Donk, Loader, Nixon, & Rucht, 2004; for a review, see Garrett, 2006).

---

[1] Paraxylene is a petrochemical feedstock used in plastics, polyester, and other synthetic manufacturing. Xiamen, Dalian, Ningbo, Kunming, and Maoming in the two messages are cities in China, and Zhenhai is a district of Ningbo.

Nevertheless, most of this scholarship tends to focus on either the analysis of discrete contentious events (e.g., McCaughey & Ayers, 2013; van de Donk et al., 2004) or the comparative analysis of similar events (e.g., Bennett & Segerberg, 2012; Castells, 2012). Such approaches fail to analyze the possible interconnections that might be found between different instances of (digitally mediated) political contention (e.g., the anti-PX protests just cited).[2] To advance such an understanding, this study employs the concept of "cycles of contention" (Tarrow, 1993a, 1993b) to explore *the recurrent mechanism* of digital activism in contemporary society. It takes the recurrent anti-PX protests in six cities in China from 2007 to 2014 as the case to examine the factors that contribute to the emergence and sustainability of assimilative digitally mediated environmental activism. This study sheds light on the enduring mechanism of digital activism and political contention in authoritarian regimes like China.

This study first presents a critical review of current studies of ICTs and political activism with a focus on digital activism in China. Second, it introduces and develops the concept of cycles of contention as the theoretical framework to scrutinize the factors that shape the mechanism of recurrence and that sustain digitally mediated political contention. Third, this study specifies case selection and overview, data collection, and methods of analysis. Fourth, it examines the mechanism that produces the recurrence of certain strategies of digitally mediated environmental activism and digital media as "repertoires of contention" (Tilly, 1986). This study concludes with thoughts on the mechanism that underpins the dynamics of digitally mediated, sustained political activism beyond a single contentious event.

DIGITAL MEDIA AND POLITICAL ACTIVISM: THE CASE OF CHINA

Scholars are increasingly discussing the ways in which digital media are being used in political activism around the world. Some explore the affordance of digital media for information distribution for political contention (e.g., Hands, 2011; Kahn & Kellner, 2004). Others underline the relevance of digital media in the process of structuring and bridging networks for collective action (e.g., Bennett & Segerberg, 2012; Biddix & Park, 2008). Some argue for digital media being a catalyst for protest organization, mobilization, and participation (e.g., Liu, 2015; Rojas & Puig-i-Abril, 2009). Others observe identity- and value-driven subpolitics as key elements in digitally mediated political activism (e.g., Bakardjieva, 2009; Yang, 2009).

---

[2] Although recognizing the interconnection, or acts of imitation within different forms of activism, most of these studies did not probe very deeply into these interconnections or acts of imitation (e.g., Bennett & Segerberg, 2012, pp. 745–747).

The impact of digital media on political activism also has become an enduring and substantial focus in the studies of ICTs in China (e.g., Yang, 2009; Zheng, 2008; for a critical review, see Qiu & Bu, 2013, p. 126). Nevertheless, the scholarship remains dominated by case studies of discrete, independent—in some cases, isolated—contentious events, the emergence of which reflects unique internal dynamics (e.g., Yang, 2009; Zheng, 2008). Although such an approach generates a fruitful understanding of the use of digital media for single, concrete contentious events, it fails to explore possible interconnections within digitally mediated political activism and, further, to recognize their long-term effects. This reflects, to a certain extent, a crucial characteristic of political activism in Chinese society where the politically sensitive authorities worked hard with a highly repressive policy against protests in order to suppress the outbreak of political contention and to prevent the dispersal of its influence to a large scale—in particular, via digital media (e.g., King, Pan, & Roberts, 2013; also see Bamman, O'Connor, & Smith, 2012; MacKinnon, 2009). In this sense, as some studies suggest, "activism in China fails to meet the definition of a 'social movement' because it is usually localized and falls short of sustained contention" (Huang & Sun, 2014, p. 87).

However, existing scholarship does observe and acknowledge that earlier political struggles affect, facilitate, or even legitimize subsequent contentious movements, consequently transgressing specific contentious events and generating a long-term influence in the society. For instance, findings of several studies on digital media and political movements suggested that early protests not only become the blueprint for later political movements but also lend "legitimacy" to later struggles (Hu, 2012; Lee & Ho, 2014; Zeng, 2015, pp. 34–35). Yang (2011) reminded readers of the "gradual revolution" in China under the influence of online political activism by proposing that "these popular political forms have already left their imprints on Chinese politics ... they add up and their cumulative effects are profound" (pp. 1044–1045). In this sense, failing to recognize the imprint of early-riser activism on latecomers and the interconnections between them leaves significant lacunae in our understanding of the sustained influence of political activism on Chinese society.

Meanwhile, social movement studies long have argued that contentious events are *hardly* discrete phenomena, independent of one another (McAdam, 1995, p. 218, also see Minkoff, 1997; Traugott, 1995). Instead, they not only share a "family resemblance" (McAdam, Tarrow, & Tilly, 2001, p. 165) but also encourage the emergence of assimilation, further lowering constraint and forming opportunities for broader and recurring contention (e.g., McAdam, 1995; Tarrow, 2010, 2011, p. 201). To go beyond a single contentious event as the unit of analysis and instead canvass the interconnection dynamics of political activism, a feasible method might be to draw on the concept of cycles of contention.

BEYOND THE SINGLE CONTENTIOUS EVENT: CYCLES OF CONTENTION

Cycles of Contention, Modular Collective Action, and Repertoires of Contention

The concept of "cycles of contention" has been coined in the works of Tarrow (1993a, 1993b) to enunciate the rolling, recurrent mechanism of protests and its contribution to longer-term changes in collective action and society at large (see also McAdam et al., 2001, pp. 65–68; Traugott, 1995). According to Tarrow (2011), a "cycle of contention" refers to:

> a phase of heightened conflict across the social system, with rapid diffusion of collective action from more mobilized to less mobilized sectors, a rapid pace of innovation in the forms of contention employed, the creation of new or transformed collective action frames, a combination of organized and unorganized participation, and sequences of intensified information flow and interaction between challengers and authorities. (p. 199)

"Cycles of contention" acts as a key term to explicate the translation of forms of collective action in moments of contention into the historical development of means for making claims and engaging in struggles in a society, known as the "repertoire of contention."

As Tilly (1995) defined it, the "repertoire of contention" is "a limited set of routines that are learned, shared, and acted out through a relatively deliberate process of choice" (p. 42). The repertoire of contention is an array of contentious claims making and performance that always is situated in prior societal experience. People learn from the history and experience of contention and then borrow or imitate these "learned conventions of contention" (Tarrow, 2011, p. 29) in later struggles. Thereby, most of the time, the tactics or forms of collective action in any given place bear a strong resemblance to previous iterations. The consequent borrowing or imitation leads to cycles of certain types of protest in a society. In this cyclical process, a stock of these inherited tactics or forms of collective action that become habitual and that transfer across different contentious contexts consequently become "the permanent tools of a society's repertoires of contention" (Tarrow, 1993a, p. 284).

A key contribution from cycles of contention to what becomes the eventual repertoire of contention is the modularization of emerging forms of struggles, which facilitates the diffusion of these forms and ultimately leads to their translation into permanent changes in the repertoire of contention. To be clear, the outcome of recurrent struggles influences the shape of the next by providing an array of possible tactics and, more important, "modular repertoires" (Tarrow,

1993a; Tilly, 1986, p. 6). The modular repertoires manifest in the capacity of forms of collective action to be used in a variety of conflicts by a number of different social actors and by coalitions of people against a variety of opponents (Tarrow, 1993b, p. 77). As such, the modularity of collective action allows for the *transferability* of repertoires into different contexts (Wada, 2012). In short, cycles of contention entail models of collective action that allow the outcome of a single moment of political activism to transcend beyond itself as such and to sustain collective challenges for subsequent participants.

Cycles of contention also bring the possibility of institutional change by engendering an indirect effect on the political opportunity structure and constraints, as people challenging authority increase the leverage of other groups to challenge authorities and elevate their own power or privilege (McAdam, 1995, pp. 221–222). In this sense, cycles generate a longer and broader influence of protest that goes beyond a discrete contentious event by diffusing, fashioning, and legitimizing forms of collective action. Accordingly, McAdam (1995) suggested that we "shift our focus of attention from discrete social movements to the broader 'movement families' or 'cycles of protest' in which they are typically embedded" (p. 218).

Organizations, Mass Media, and Diffusion of Contention

A key element to facilitate cycles of contention is the diffusion of contention, which allows "word of successful—and learnable—collective actions" to be spread to more groups and localities for mimetic struggles and "be sustained far longer than the episodic and cathartic collective actions of the past" (Tarrow, 1993b, p. 82). Some studies recognize the relevance of organizations (e.g., Social Movement Organizations) or associational networks in the process of distributing information in established networks as a precondition for diffusion (McAdam, 1995, p. 232; Minkoff, 1997). Others observe the significance of the media in the process of disseminating the news about protests beyond their immediate social settings (Oliver & Myers, 1999, p. 39). Studies recount that mass media play a critical role in the progression of protest cycles by broadcasting action strategies to potential adopters, connecting otherwise unconnected individuals via a shared response to events, shaping the public opinion and framing of contention issues, and routinizing protests as institutionalized politics (for detailed discussions, see Gamson & Wolfsfeld, 1993; Oliver & Maney, 2000; Oliver & Myers, 1999; Tarrow, 2011, p. 201).

Research findings increasingly suggest that digital media such as the internet facilitates the transfer of "protest ideas and tactics quickly and efficiently across national borders" (Norris, 2002, p. 208). Boyle and Schmierbach (2009) dissected the emerging role of alternative media (i.e., the web) in prompting both traditional and protest participation. Tufekci and Wilson (2012) discussed how sharing prior personal protest experiences via social media drove the follow-up protests in Egypt.

Nevertheless, current studies are largely based on protests in Western democracies, and they fail to consider the diffusion of—and thereby the cycles of—contention in highly controlled authoritarian regimes like China. The Chinese government works hard to impose a tightening of state control over both traditional and digital media. The diffusion of information on protests especially suffers from intensive suppression (e.g., King et al., 2013). Meanwhile, findings of several studies suggest that social organizations, such as environmental non-governmental organizations, have been missing in the process of political activism, largely due to political pressure and surveillance (Wu & Wen, 2015, p. 113). How can the diffusion and further cycles of contention develop in a highly controlled, politically sensitive context in which both protest information and social organizations have been under strict governmental control? Such a context makes China a relevant case to understand the *recurrent dynamics* of political activism. The overarching research question becomes, What specific factors and processes account for the recurrent dynamics of digital activism in a highly controlled context such as China?

I respond to this overarching query with three research questions:

RQ1: How do people get information about protests—including information about political activism of the past and present?
RQ2: What are the factors that contribute to people's perception of digital media as the repertoire of contention?
RQ3: What are the processes—for example, diffusion of knowledge about protests —by which earlier movements facilitate follow-up activism and further generate cycles of contention?

METHODS

The study examines seven anti-PX protests in six cities from 2007 to 2014. Starting with the anti-PX protest in Xiamen in 2007, PX has become a common target for public protest and environmental activism in China. Since then, as a result of public discontent, anti-PX protests have broken out in several cities including, chronologically, Chengdu in 2008, Dalian in 2011, Ningbo in 2012, Kunming and Chengdu in 2013, and Maoming in 2014.[3] Among them, some cities are known for their peace and quiet, rarely witnessing protests (e.g., Xiamen and Kunming). The process also consists of varied social groups, including students, intellectuals, and villagers, as well as journalists, police, professionals, and other types of urbanites (e.g., the

---

[3] Nevertheless, this does not mean that interconnection exists only between the anti-PX protests. Rather, people were inspired by the anti-PX protests and imitated them in other instances of political activism; see, for instance, Hu (2012, p. 104).

middle class in Xiamen, Dalian, and Kunming). In short, the original anti-PX protest has grown into one of the most prominent, recurrent forms of environmental activism in contemporary China.

More important, the anti-PX protests have witnessed the adoption and appropriation of digital media as an indispensable means of political activism. As early as 2007, people largely relied on mobile communication to organize the anti-PX protest in Xiamen (Liu, 2013). In subsequent protests, people continued to exploit various digital media to galvanize protests, including internet forums, QQ, *weibo*, text messaging, and WeChat, where protestors shared information and protest plans, as well as facilitated collective action mobilization (e.g., Sevastopulo, 2014). Photos, videos, and on-the-spot reports of the protests have also spread in real-time via, for instance, *weibo*, WeChat, Facebook, and Twitter. The anti-PX protests thus allow us to observe the integration of digital media into environmental activism and its possible contribution to the sustainability of environmental activism.

From these cases, I used snowball sampling and in-depth interviews with protest participants to explore both the diffusion of protests over the course of political activism and perception of digital media as a repertoire of contention. In China's tightly controlled and monitored political environment, the distribution of protest information is strictly prohibited, as is personal participation in the protest. The snowball sampling allowed the researcher to identify and recruit "hidden populations," or individuals or groups that are not easily accessible through other sampling strategies (Salganik & Heckathorn, 2004). To access the hidden populations of protestors in these cases, I identified three to five participants in six cities and asked them to provide contact information for three to five persons they met during protests, from whom they received protest information, or to whom they delivered the information. This process aims to discover as many protest participants as possible. I replicated this process to recruit additional research participants. This network-based sampling procedure guaranteed the interviewees' privacy and ensured that their participation in protests would be kept to a low profile. Of the initial 85 participants contacted for the study, 54 agreed to be interviewed. The interviewees were an average age of 35.7 years old. Eighty-three percent of them (45 of 54) had a bachelor's degree, or higher, but all were internet users who were familiar with digital media in various forms. The professions of the interviewees included journalist, editor, graduate student, high school student, lawyer, sales representative, consultant, university lecturer, taxi driver, IT professional, mobile phone salesperson, barber, and small clothing store owner. Fifty interviewees physically participated in the protests, whereas four participants attended the protests "virtually"—they were engaged in the distribution of protest information via online forums and social networking sites (e.g., Facebook and *weibo*). The interviewees all shared a firm understanding of ICTs as a relevant means of anti-PX protests. Such an understanding is relevant for the analysis of the perception of digital media as a repertoire of contention.

I conducted semistructured in-depth interviews, following the direction and general framework of the interview while eliciting detailed responses and probing when clarification was necessary. In particular, I adhered to the notion that "the repertoire is not only what people *do* ... it is what they *know how to do* and what others *expect* them to do" (Tarrow, 1993b, p. 70, emphasis in original). Questions in the interview guide thereby included not only the use of digital media for protests but also how the interviewees *knew* and *perceived* digital media as a means of struggle; what kind of experience or knowledge they had for the protests; where this experience or knowledge came from; and how it was gained, justified, and validated via which channel.

The interviews lasted 1.5 hours. Of the 54 interviews, I conducted 48 face-to-face by traveling to the cities where the interviewees resided and the remaining six via Gmail due to a concern about government surveillance of social media and e-mail communication. I conducted all interviews in Chinese and in person, which I then transcribed and translated. I documented interviews only when the interviewee was comfortable and anonymity could be guaranteed.

After data collection, I employed thematic analysis and cross-case synthesis (Yin, 2009, p. 18) to determine which factors contributed to and further sustained the diffusion and recurrence of environmental protests.

FINDINGS

This section presents the findings from the interviews about the diffusion of contention and the perception of digital media as a means of contention. Findings from the interviews demonstrate that diffusion emerges from social and group-based applications of digital media and then spreads to other digital media platforms. Following that, traditional media such as newspapers and television start to publish news about protests. Both traditional and digital media contribute to the diffusion of information about anti-PX protests for political activism, but accomplish this in distinct ways.

Diffusion of Contention via Digital Media

In an atmosphere where both mass media and social organizations are under highly repressive control, digital media act as a crucial channel for people to distribute and receive information regarding (a) politically sensitive issues (e.g., PX); (b) collective action mobilization; and (c) collective action of the past, which enables people to learn from earlier experiences.

According to the interviews, people categorized various digital media into two segments: One includes social and group-based applications of digital media, such as QQ, WeChat, and mobile phones; the other was digital media platforms such as *weibo*, web pages, and online forums. First, social and group-based applications of digital media served as the primary source of relevant but politically sensitive information—PX-related information in this case. In practice, 94% (51 of 54) of interviewees said that the information about the PX project emerged and circulated within their social networks via mobile call, text messaging, QQ, and WeChat. The rest received the information via face-to-face interaction and from their digitally mediated social networks. For instance, several participants in the Xiamen case recalled that around three months before the protest, they started to receive "a warning text message regarding the PX project"[4] from their friends, colleagues, and relatives, which was the first time they heard the name "PX." The text message ran rampant within a short time, whereas, according to a 35-year-old taxi driver, "local media did not mention this issue at all for over 3 months." Against this backdrop, reportedly, the phrase "did you receive the [PX-related] SMS?" became the opening remark when Xiamen residents met each other during this 3-month period (Zhu, 2007). In this sense, it is the information from mobile social networks that informed people and initiated further discussion about the project.

If Xiamen residents basically relied on text messaging to receive and spread PX information, later protests adopted various social network–based digital media for the same purpose. In the cases of Kunming, Chengdu, and Maoming, local residents mostly used QQ and WeChat to disseminate PX information, inform their social networks, and initiate discussions, even if traditional media did not cover the issue at all. In other words, people no longer had to depend on traditional media as a key information source.

Second, in addition to the diffusion of PX-related information, people also spread mobilizing messages for "strolls" (*sanbu*), a euphemism they used for street protests, via social and group-based applications of digital media. In the Xiamen case, the mobilizing message had been disseminated largely via mobile communication. Similarly, as listed earlier in this article, the messages calling for protests proliferated via digital media and fundamentally turned into a key part of the mechanism of mobilization in the cases of Ningbo and Maoming.

It is important to note that such information got *immediate attention and action* from people, as it came from their (digitally mediated) social networks. A 43-year-old IT engineer from the Maoming case explained, "It [the message] came from someone you know, you trust, and you care about. ... That means it [the message] is relevant; it is urgent. It is an appeal from your social network that asks for your immediate response."

---

[4] For the detailed information of the text message, see Xie and Zhao (2007).

This statement shows that the embedding of social relations into the process of digitally mediated mobilization exerts an essential influence on people's attitudes toward the message they received and triggers immediate, follow-up action. They were inspired to distribute the message widely in their digitally mediated social networks and to search for further information about PX, for instance, via search engines and in *weibo*. These actions furthered the swift diffusion of protest information throughout society and inspired collective action.

More specifically, the easy-to-use feature of digital media allows people to invite their social networks into collective action mobilization without much effort. A 23-year-old graduate from the Kunming case said that she had forwarded the message via WeChat to her whole class and her relatives, a total of 75 people, by "just twiddling the thumb." In the Xiamen case, the apex of the anti-PX movement occurred as "millions of Xiamen residents frenziedly forward[ed] the same [mobilizing] text message around their mobile phones" (Lan & Zhang, 2007), urging each other to join a street protest opposing the government's PX project. The interviewees from other cases also confirmed that they had forwarded such mobilizing messages to different social groups with which they were affiliated by "copying," "pasting," and "sending" the message or simply pressing the "forward" or "retweet" button. The easy-to-use digital devices with inexpensive telecommunication fees for information dissemination became the key facilitator—be it through text messaging, QQ, or WeChat—to mobilize as many people as possible into the protest.

Third, people moved to search engines, microblogging sites, and online forums to look for information about PX after receiving the message from their digitally mediated social networks. These digital platforms became major channels for them to explore more detailed information about the issues they were concerned with and, more important, to retrieve information about previous protests concerning these issues in order to learn from them. The interviewees reported that they found a lot of information on anti-PX protests in other cities as soon as they searched keywords such as "PX" via digital media. Then they read and learned from these past experiences. A 33-year-old clothing store owner from Ningbo described it thus:

> You can find web pages, online forums, and tweets including photos and videos of the anti-PX protest in Xiamen, the very first one in 2007. These contents expand our awareness of the PX project. ... It shows to us the way we can adapt to stop the project.

Although the protest in Xiamen remained "the most renowned anti-PX protest," according to a 27-year-old mobile phone salesperson from Chengdu, people can also easily retrieve news, photos, and videos about later ones in

Kunming, Dalian, and so on, from web pages, microblogging, blogs, and online forums despite censorship. She said,

> After checking the internet, we saw several anti-PX protests around the nation. If the project is not toxic or problematic [as the government declared], why would people in other cities oppose it? Why do we need a project that people elsewhere discarded? If they [people in other cities] succeeded in forcing the government to give up the project by protests, we should also do the same!

Although such "reasoning" did not convert into offline protest action *directly*, it did encourage people to redistribute the information via digital media within their social networks. As soon as these messages had been spread via diverse digital platforms, they multiplied within a very short time and spread to services beyond the control of state censors. For one thing, the messages diffused through decentralized network infrastructure before the government recognized it and initiated censorship. For another, the rapid and widespread diffusion of these messages made it impossible for the government to eliminate them completely. In this way, information about the anti-PX protests proliferated within digitally mediated social networks, allowing as many people as possible to know and learn from these experiences.

To sum up, both social and group-based digital media and web pages, online forums, and microblogs, became a crucial channel of the diffusion of protest information, which includes both mobilizing messages and the past experiences of protests. The social and group-based applications of digital media enable people to distribute information that demands immediate attention and action as quickly and as widely as possible. Meanwhile, web pages, online forums, and microblogs provided abundant information, especially about previous protests. Such information greatly shaped people's perception about the PX project and laid the foundation for further contention.

Coverage and Diffusion of Contention via Traditional Media

People also read the information about the PX project, the ensuing debate, and the coverage of anti-PX protests in traditional media. According to the interviews, traditional media refers to the state-controlled media, such as newspapers and television. In general, the information from traditional media is designed to persuade the public to accept the PX project by citing professional opinions or by claiming that ill-intended protesters falsified or exaggerated the toxicity of PX to mislead the public. Of interest, the information from traditional media failed to change attitudes toward the project. Instead, it enriched knowledge of the protests, provided successful, learnable examples to follow, and acted as a *deterministic* element to encourage adoption of digital media for protests.

First, traditional media's coverage of the controversies and objections against the PX project services acted as a catalyst to ignite widespread contention against the project, as people perceived the emergence of the coverage as both the removal of censorship and an admission of the danger of the PX project by the authorities. In practice, traditional media's coverage of PX-related information did not turn up until the information proliferated within social and group-based digital media. For instance, local media in Xiamen started to cover the PX project only after the controversies spread via mobile phones for around three months. Meanwhile, the authorities worked hard from the beginning to censor sensitive words such as "PX" and "petrochemical," shutting down online forums that contained arguments against the project and blocking access to overseas coverage of this issue. Nevertheless, facing the proliferation of PX-related information via digital media and the coverage by international media, traditional media also started to cover the debate. This significant change was perceived as the cessation of censorship regarding the debate over PX. The interviews showed that people believed that, following the traditional media coverage, they were allowed to argue against the PX project publicly. A 38-year-old IT professional said, "Even the government had to admit the detriment of the PX project in [mass] media! Why can't we oppose it?"

Second, the traditional media coverage on the anti-PX protest encouraged people to learn and imitate earlier collective actions—in particular, the successful "stroll" in Xiamen—against the project. According to the interviews, official media, such as *People's Daily*, the official newspaper of the Communist Party of China; *China Newsweek*, published by China News Service, the second-largest state news agency; and national and regional level newspapers such as *Southern Metropolis Daily* covered the anti-PX protests. To them, the coverage implied that "the (central) government had accepted 'the stroll,' or street protest, as a legit way of opposing the PX project" (said a 36-year-old taxi driver from the Chengdu case). As an authorized symbol (O'Brien, 1996, p. 37) from the central government, the coverage became not only a benchmark of anti-PX protest but also a successful, politically accepted example for people elsewhere to learn, follow, and duplicate later. For instance, a 42-year-old university lecturer from the Kunming case explained,

> The media will not be allowed to cover the protest in Xiamen if it is an illegal act. Now it [the protest] appears in the news, which means the government recognized this activity as a legitimate form of public participation in the PX issue. … We can take to the streets as people in Xiamen did [to march against the PX project].

Third, traditional media's coverage plays a key role to influence the adoption of digital media for protests. The way these media covered anti-PX protests underlined the relevant role of digital media in initiating and organizing protests, serving as examples for people to learn from the past by adopting and appropriating various digital media for protests. For instance, the interviewees from several cases mentioned a report by *China Newsweek*. Titled "The Power of Mobile Messaging" (Xie & Zhao, 2007), the report detailed how Xiamen residents used text messaging to organize the anti-PX protest. People treated this report as a signal from the authorities giving *tacit consent* to using mobile phones for successful protest organization. A 36-year-old accountant from the Chengdu case recalled,

> Even the central authorities acknowledged the power of mobile phones for successful protest. We can copy the "stroll" in Xiamen by using our mobile phones to organize similar protests against the PX project. This successful example shows a way recognized by the government to oppose the project.

Similarly, in later coverage on the anti-PX protests, traditional media reported the use of various digital media as tools for protest, which consequently becomes the main driving force that inspires and encourages the "replication" of successful examples of the past by employing digital media for protest.

To sum up, traditional media played a key role in shaping knowledge of past protests, which facilitated digitally mediated protests against the PX project. Although *none* of these reports said that the protests were legal, media coverage was considered to be a withdrawal of censorship over opposition against PX, the go-ahead signal for protest activity. Similarly, the way these reports covered the anti-PX protest played a fundamental role in shaping attitudes and actions against the project. The coverage of the use of digital media was perceived as an encouragement to follow "the successful model" of the past by adopting digital media for political contention. These events have sustained the digitally mediated anti-PX protests.

DISCUSSION

In a series of recurring protests against PX projects from 2007 to 2014, this study's findings suggest that both digital and traditional media facilitate the diffusion of contention and contribute to the mechanism of recurrence, but in two distinct ways. The affordances of digital media, such as ease of use, immediacy, and the embedding of social networks, generate a process of *mass self-mobilization*, through which people disseminate protest information as quickly and widely as possible; more important, it allows them to rapidly engage in collective action mobilization. In this process, the rapid and wide dissemination by virtue of digital media allows the past experience of collective action to be available and accessible to the public to learn, duplicate, and adopt in practice despite censorship. Further, the coverage of contention by traditional, official media not only *legitimizes* but also *modularizes* the contention, further encouraging the emergence of assimilation. More important, traditional media play a crucial role in shaping perception of digital media as a repertoire of contention, which leads to the sustainability of digitally mediated political contention. Next, I explore the different contributions of digital and traditional media in terms of the diffusion, legitimation, and modularity of contention, respectively, followed by a discussion of digital media as a repertoire of contention and the sustainability of anti-PX protests as an example of environmental activism in contemporary China.

Digital Media, Diffusion of Contention, and Mass Self-Mobilization

Due to the fear of the contagion effect of protests, the Chinese government struggles to detect and eradicate collective action information as it emerges. Against this backdrop, digital media serve as a key resource of the diffusion of contention against censorship. More specifically, the unique affordances of digital media, including availability, accessibility, and affordability, facilitate the proliferation of information without the engagement of traditional media and generate a process of what I call "mass self-mobilization."

First, availability indicates that low-end ICTs have become a simple yet substantial necessity for everyday life, which institutes the adoption of digital media as a quotidian tool for political activism. In China, the population of mobile phone users surpassed 1.2 billion, or 94% of its total population, in 2014. The mobile messaging app WeChat has more than 500 million active users monthly. More than 290 million *weibo* users account for 45.9% of the total 632 million Chinese internet users in 2014 (CNNIC, 2014). Due to the lack of institutional support and resources for political contention under authoritarian control, people appropriate and largely rely on their digital media, a communication tool, to initiate and facilitate collective action (e.g., Huang & Sun, 2014; Yang, 2009). Similarly, cases examined here show that the Chinese public takes advantage of digital media as the most readily available resource for protest distribution, organization, and mobilization.

Second, ease of use and low cost contribute to the accessibility and affordability of digital media—in particular, social and group-based applications of digital media—which allows instant dissemination of protest information and collective action mobilization to occur and renders digital media a key resource for both informing and uniting individuals, even those who have little technological know-how. As the interviews exemplify, digital media allow people to spread politically sensitive messages, initiate collective action, or resist authority through a simple method—for instance, "twiddling their thumbs" on a mobile phone—to promote political activism. Meanwhile, with instant communication, digital media enable the release of contentious information at the flick of a button, be it through mobile phones or personal computers. In this way, the diffusion of contention, including past experience of struggles, easily transcends geographic boundaries and facilitates large-scale impact (e.g., international news coverage), leaving the government unable to cover up either the contested issue (i.e., the PX project) or the politically sensitive one (e.g., protest). Such diffusion is so relevant that it enables people, in varying degrees, to draw their impetus and inspiration from the collective action of the past.

Moreover, digital media deliver calls to act on the basis of social networks; in other words, they incorporate social relationship as the mobilization agent, which in turn becomes the driving force for engaging in both information dissemination and collective action mobilization. In this process, as we have observed elsewhere (e.g., Bennett & Segerberg, 2012; Liu, 2015), the digital technology affordances activate and articulate social networks for political contention. With help from digital media, the threshold for initiating, engaging, promoting, or supporting political action becomes low.

These affordances contribute to a process of mass self-mobilization, which is inspired by Castells's (2009) phrase "mass self-communication" (p. 55). In particular, the concept underlines a *quasi*-mass communication process on the basis of horizontal networks of digitally mediated interactive communication *without* mass media and organizational foundation. In the case of anti-PX protests, digital media first enable people to initiate a communication process through which they distribute protest information and send messages as individuals. Next, digital media promote the practice of collective action mobilization. The term "self-mobilization" thereby goes one step further than self-communication by addressing the organizational process through which individuals, largely depending on their digital media, choose and mobilize by themselves those within their social networks. This process occurs when many circulate mobilizing messages spontaneously within their social networks. Consequently, digital media drive mass mobilization through interpersonal interactive practices in collective actions even without social organizations, transforming a means of interpersonal interaction into a mass-mobilizing tool. This point is relevant to understanding the digitally mediated process of collective action organization in the absence of social organizations, including social movement organizations, in authoritarian regimes.

Traditional Media and the Legitimation and Modularity of Contention

In a repressive political environment such as China, political contention normally faces great political risk and encounters harsh political suppression by the state (e.g., O'Brien, 2009). Against this backdrop, the mere diffusion of contention— or, simply knowing about the protest—is not enough to inspire political activism. Instead, people exploit official ideologies through, for instance, "the innovative use of laws, policies, and other officially promoted values" (O'Brien, 1996, p. 32) to legitimate their resistance and protest (also see O'Brien & Li, 2006). In the case of the anti-PX protests, although digital media facilitate the diffusion and mobilization of contention, it is the traditional official media that legitimize and modularize the contention, further encouraging the emergence of assimilation in the long run.

First, traditional media's coverage increases the influence of the anti-PX protests by legitimizing the protest as a kind of "partially sanctioned resistance" (O'Brien, 1996, p. 33) and consequently encouraging widespread duplication. O'Brien (1996) noted in the study of rural contention that increased media penetration cultivated villagers to be "more knowledgeable about resistance routines devised elsewhere" (p. 41). In the case of anti-PX protests, the government exerted censorship over PX-related information at the beginning, then later removed the censorship and allowed traditional media to cover the issue, including the protest. To the average person, the coverage of anti-PX protests implied that the controversies around the PX project were no longer a political taboo as soon as traditional media began to cover them. Instead, the authorities recognized its existence, allowing people to openly discuss and, more important, accept the protest as legitimate. In other words, as the interviews show, the anti-PX protests have been recognized as "a form of officially legitimate public action" (Thireau & Linshan, 2003, p. 87) in the general public (see Oliver & Myers, 1999, p. 44–45). The coverage by national mass media (e.g., *China Newsweek*), beyond the control of local authorities but considered as "an extension of state power" (Shi & Cai, 2006, p. 329), significantly persuaded locals that their protest against local authorities' decision on the PX project had been tolerated and accepted with the connivance of the central authority, thereby establishing opportunities for later contention. This "schemata of interpretations" (Zhao, 2010, p. 42) perceived and shared by the public as a significant institutional policy change regarding the PX project consequently expanded political opportunities for contention and encouraged the adoption of such a form of collective action against PX projects for successors elsewhere.

It is also necessary to address the anti-PX protests as a specific form of environmental activism in contemporary China. By addressing its specificity, I mean the protest—and environmental activism in general—is tolerated by the authorities because it largely concerns environmental issues and does not challenge the authoritarian role (also see Zhao, 2010, p. 45). As Yang and Calhoun (2007) emphasized, the emergence of "a green public sphere of critical environmental discourse" (p. 211) with a growth of environmental nongovernmental organizations and a diversity of localized environmental movements in response to the rise of the environmental crisis since the early 1990s is *distinctive*, because "it engages politics and public policy without being primarily political" (Yang & Calhoun, 2007, p.212; also see Sullivan & Xie, 2009; Yang, 2005, 2007). This fundamentally lowers the political risk of the protest itself, as well as that of the media to cover the protest.

Second, traditional media detail and highlight the use of digital media for protests, which leads to the modularity of anti-PX activism and further encourages imitation by latecomers. For instance, the interviewees recalled clearly that *China Newsweek* dedicated its cover story to the use of text messaging in the anti-PX protest in Xiamen. The reports described in detail how people used their mobile phones to distribute "millions of messages" for protest mobilization (Xie & Zhao, 2007, p. 16). Similarly, later reports included the way in which people employed various digital media, such as QQ, online forums, and WeChat, to organize protests successfully (The Center for Public Opinion Monitor, 2014; Zeng, 2015, pp. 112–113). In this way, traditional media covered the anti-PX protests and addressed the adoption of digital media as a unique and successful aspect of the protest. As news about this form of digitally mediated collective action spread, it generated a demonstration effect of the anti-PX protest by offering key tactics as "mobilizing information" (Lemert, 1984, p. 244). According to the interviews, the anti-PX protest has become a typical, successful model that crystallizes digital activism in the process of struggling against authority, finally forcing it to change its decision. In this way, news coverage consequently modularizes the digitally mediated anti-PX protest as a successful example of protest organization and an established pattern of political engagement. The modularity of anti-PX protests accordingly establishes and facilitates patterns of digitally mediated contentious behaviors that "can be learned, adapted, routinized, and diffused from one group, one locale, or one moment to another" (Traugott, 1995, p. 7). The tactical and organizational means and strategies that earlier anti-PX protests employed further afford later struggles. Thus, the coverage and diffusion by traditional media allow people to adopt modes of contention easily by learning from the past and duplicating it, facilitating its transferability into other cases, and furthering the popular perception of digital media as *a repertoire of contention* in society.

Digital Media as a Repertoire of Contention and the Sustainability of Anti-Px Protests

The contention repertoire involves specifically what people *know* how to do in contention (Tarrow, 2011, p. 39). Here, repertoire derives from the learned experience of the contested means of the past. In a series of anti-PX protests, a key contribution from traditional media to the recurrent mechanism of anti-PX protests is the establishment of the perception of digital media as a repertoire of contention. More specifically, it is the emphasis on digital media, be it text messaging or WeChat, in traditional media that leaves an impression binding anti-PX protests and the adoption of digital media together. As the interviews show, the coverage of protests by traditional media establishes a framework in which digital media as a flexible and well-understood means of making claims and opposing others becomes a key option of these repertoires of contention. As people read the news coverage of anti-PX protests, this coverage becomes the "guideline" for people to duplicate the previous protest by adopting digital media as a means of engaging and spreading political contention. To the public, the power of mobile messaging not only depicts the political influence of mobile technologies but also serves as a slogan to encourage people to adopt their digital media for protests. In this way, traditional media play a key role by inspiring use of digital media for activism and as a repertoire of contention.

CONCLUSION

Different from most current studies on political activism with focuses on a singular contentious event, this study underlines the interconnections between instances of contention by employing the concept "cycles of contention" to investigate the recurrent mechanism of anti-PX protests in contemporary China. I argue that digital media play a key role in informing people about the contention. But it is the traditional media that legitimize and modularize contention and encourage the emergence of repeated patterns of collective action. In this sense, the intertwining of digital media and traditional media generates the recurrent dynamics of contention and sustains the long-term influence of digitally mediated environmental activism in China.

This study advances the understanding of (digitally) mediated political activism in the following three perspectives: First, it depicts a nuanced picture about the distinct contributions from digital media and traditional media to the recurrent mechanism of contention. As this study argues, for the sustainability of political activism in authoritarian regimes such as China, it is not enough to have digital media or traditional media alone. Various types of media contribute to different elements of the recurrent mechanism.

Second, this study emphasizes the legitimation and modularity of contention as a key contribution from traditional media where repressive political policies discourage the emergence of contention. The prominence and success of political activism in official media do, in fact, promote learnable forms of struggle, expand political opportunities, and sustain political contention in a politically repressive context. This study resonates with Tarrow's (1993b) argument that "it was in the shadow of the national state that social movements developed their characteristic modular forms of collective action" (p. 85).

I propose that by integrating the concept of "cycles of contention" into study of political activism, better understanding of contentious events emerges from the investigation of the historicity of the contention. As this study demonstrates, the historicity of political activism articulates the legacies of the past as *the very conditions* that constitute present political activism.

ACKNOWLEDGMENTS

I appreciate the comments from Klaus Bruhn Jensen, Ran Wei, and two anonymous reviewers.

FUNDING

This work was supported by the Carlsberg Foundation [grant number CF14-0385]; S. C. Van Fonden [reference numbers 1267, 1503].

REFERENCES

Bakardjieva, M. (2009). Subactivism. *The Information Society, 25*(2), 91–104.

Bamman, D., O'Connor, B., & Smith, N. (2012). Censorship and deletion practices in Chinese social media. *First Monday, 17*(3). Retrieved from http://firstmonday.org/ojs/index.php/fm/article/view/3943/3169

BBC. (2014, April 2). *China Maoming environmental protest violence condemned.* Retrieved from http://www.bbc.com/news/world-asia-china-26849814

Bennett, W. L., & Segerberg, A. (2012). The logic of connective action. *Information, Communication & Society, 15*(5), 739–768.

Biddix, J. P., & Park, H. W. (2008). Online networks of student protest. *New Media & Society, 10*(6), 871–891.

Boyle, M. P., & Schmierbach, M. (2009). Media use and protest. *Communication Quarterly, 57*(1), 1–17.

Castells, M. (2009). *Communication power.* Oxford, UK: Oxford University Press.

Castells, M. (2012). *Networks of outrage and hope.* Cambridge, MA: Polity.

Chang, M. (2013, May 17). Thousands protest Kunming PX plan. *Global Times.* Retrieved from http://www.globaltimes.cn/content/782252.shtml

CNNIC. (2014, July). *The 34th statistics report on internet development in China.* Retrieved from http://www1.cnnic.cn/IDR/ReportDownloads/201411/P020141102574314897888.pdf

Earl, J., & Kimport, K. (2011). *Digitally enabled social change.* Cambridge, MA: MIT Press.

FlorCruz, J. A. (2012, July 6). *People power a sign of times in China's internet age.* Retrieved from http://edition.cnn.com/2012/07/06/world/asia/china-shifang-protest-florcruz/

Gamson, W. A., & Wolfsfeld, G. (1993). Movements and media as interacting systems. *The Annals of the American Academy of Political and Social Science, 528,* 114–125.

Garrett, R. K. (2006). Protest in an information society. *Information, Communication and Society, 9*(2), 202–224.

Hands, J. (2011). *@ is for Activism.* London, UK: Pluto Press.

Hu, Y. (2012). The Internet and social mobilization in China. In F. L. Lee, L. Leung, J. L. Qiu, & D. S. Chu (Eds.), *Frontiers in new media research* (pp. 93–114). London, UK: Routledge.

Huang, R., & Sun, X. (2014). Weibo network, information diffusion and implications for collective action in China. *Information, Communication & Society, 17*(1), 86–104.

Kahn, R., & Kellner, D. (2004). New media and internet activism. *New Media & Society, 6*(1), 87–95.

King, G., Pan, J., & Roberts, M. E. (2013). How censorship in China allows government criticism but silences collective expression. *American Political Science Review, 107*(2), 1–18.

Lan, Y., & Zhang, Y. (2007, May 29). Millions of Xiamen residents spread crazily the same SMS to against high-pollution project. *Southern Metropolis Daily*. Retrieved from http://news.hsw.cn/2007-05/29/content_6311487.htm

Lee, K., & Ho, M.-S. (2014). The Maoming anti-PX protest of 2014. *China Perspectives, 3*, 33–39.

Lemert, J. B. (1984). News context and the elimination of mobilizing information. *Journalism Quarterly, 61*(2), 243.

Liu, D., & Yan, S. (2012, October 29). Ningbo backs down from PX project. *Global Times*. Retrieved from http://www.globaltimes.cn/content/740943.shtml

Liu, J. (2013). Mobile communication, popular protests and citizenship in China. *Modern Asian Studies, 47*(3), 995–1018.

Liu, J. (2015). Communicating beyond information. *Television & New Media, 16*(6), 503–520.

MacKinnon, R. (2009). China's Censorship 2.0. *First Monday, 14*(2). Retrieved from http://firstmonday.org/ojs/index.php/fm/article/view/3943/3169

McAdam, D. (1995). "Initiator" and "Spin-off" movements. In M. Traugott (Ed.), *Repertoires and cycles of collective action* (pp. 217–239). Durham, NC: Duke University Press.

McAdam, D., Tarrow, S. G., & Tilly, C. (2001). *Dynamics of contention*. Cambridge, UK: Cambridge University Press.

McCaughey, M., & Ayers, M. D. (2013). *Cyberactivism*. London, UK: Routledge.

Minkoff, D. C. (1997). The sequencing of social movements. *American Sociological Review, 62*(5), 779–799.

Norris, P. (2002). *Democratic phoenix*. Cambridge, UK: Cambridge University Press.

O'Brien, K. J. (1996). Rightful resistance. *World Politics, 49*(1), 31–55.

O'Brien, K. J. (2009). *Popular protest in China*. Cambridge, MA: Harvard University Press.

O'Brien, K. J., & Li, L. (2006). *Rightful resistance in rural China*. New York, NY: Cambridge University Press.

Oliver, P. E., & Maney, G. M. (2000). Political processes and local newspaper coverage of protest events. *American Journal of Sociology, 106*(2), 463–505.

Oliver, P. E., & Myers, D. J. (1999). How events enter the public sphere. *American Journal of Sociology, 105*(1), 38–87.

Qiu, J. L., & Bu, W. (2013). China ICT studies. *China Review, 13*(2), 123–152.

Rojas, H., & Puig-i-Abril, E. (2009). Mobilizers mobilized. *Journal of Computer-Mediated Communication, 14*(4), 902–927.

Salganik, M. J., & Heckathorn, D. D. (2004). Sampling and estimation in hidden populations using Respondent-Driven Sampling. *Sociological Methodology, 34*(1), 193–240.

Sevastopulo, D. (2014, April 1). China PX plant protests spread to provincial capital Guangzhou. *Financial Times*. Retrieved from http://www.ft.com/intl/cms/s/0/cf6594fa-b98d-11e3-957a-00144feabdc0.html-axzz3ZeGWgZ3k

Shi, F., & Cai, Y. (2006). Disaggregating the state. *The China Quarterly, 186*, 314–332.

Sullivan, J., & Xie, L. (2009). Environmental activism, social networks and the internet. *The China Quarterly, 198*, 422–432.

Tarrow, S. (1993a). Cycles of collective action. *Social Science History, 17*(2), 281–307.

Tarrow, S. (1993b). Modular collective action and the rise of the social movement. *Politics & Society, 21*(1), 69–90.

Tarrow, S. (2010). Dynamics of diffusion. In R. K. Givan, K. M. Roberts, & S. A. Soule (Eds.), *The diffusion of social movements* (pp. 204–219). Cambridge, UK: Cambridge University Press.

Tarrow, S. G. (2011). *Power in movement* (3rd ed.). New York, NY: Cambridge University Press.

The Center for Public Opinion Monitor. (2014). To guide the public opinion toward PX project in the Maoming protest. *Public Opinion on Politics and Law, 114*(14), 3–8.

Thireau, I., & Linshan, H. (2003). The moral universe of aggrieved Chinese workers. *The China Journal, 50*, 83–103.

Tilly, C. (1986). *The contentious French*. Cambridge, MA: Harvard University Press.

Tilly, C. (1995). *Popular contention in Great Britain, 1758-1834*. Cambridge, MA: Harvard University Press.

Traugott, M. (1995). *Repertoires and cycles of collective action*. Durham, NC: Duke University Press.

Tufekci, Z., & Wilson, C. (2012). Social media and the decision to participate in political protest. *Journal of Communication, 62*(2), 363–379.

van de Donk, W., Loader, B. D., Nixon, P. G., & Rucht, D. (Eds.). (2004). *Cyberprotest*. London, UK: Routledge.

Wada, T. (2012). Modularity and transferability of repertoires of contention. *Social Problems, 59*(4), 544–571.

Wu, F., & Wen, B. (2015). Nongovernmental organizations and environmental protests. In P. G. Harris & G. Lang (Eds.), *Routledge handbook of environment and society in Asia* (pp. 105–119). London, UK: Routledge.

Xie, L., & Zhao, L. (2007). The power of mobile messaging. *China Newsweek, 326*(20), 16–17.

Yang, G. (2005). Environmental NGOs and institutional dynamics in China. *The China Quarterly, 181*, 46–66.

Yang, G. (2009). *The power of the Internet in China*. New York, NY: Columbia University Press.

Yang, G. (2011). Technology and its contents. *The Journal of Asian Studies, 70*(4), 1043–1050.

Yang, G., & Calhoun, C. (2007). Media, civil society, and the rise of a green public sphere in China. *China Information, 21*(2), 211–236.

Yin, R. (2009). *Case study research* (4th ed.). London, UK: Sage.

Zhao, D. (2010). Theorizing the role of culture in social movements. *Social Movement Studies, 9*(1), 33–50.

Zheng, F. (2015). Diffusion effects of Chinese environmental contentions. *Journal of Northwest Normal University (Social Sciences Edition), 52*, 110–115.

Zheng, Y. (2008). *Technological empowerment*. Stanford, CA: Stanford University Press.

Zhu, H. (2007, May 30). Xiamen calls an abrupt halt to the PX project to deal with the public crisis. *Southern Weekend*, p. A1.

Media's Role in Enhancing Sustainable Development in Zambia

Carrie Young and Katherine McComas

Department of Communication
Cornell University

The dual pressures of climate change and population growth in Africa make enhancing sustainable development an important focus of initiatives hoping to reach as many people as possible with appropriate innovations. Resource and infrastructure challenges often limit the ability of programs to expand through the use of extension and other forms of in-person training. Although media such as radio, television, and mobile phones cannot replace the value of interpersonal communication, they can offer a low-cost alternative for reaching large audiences in even some of the most remote regions. With the increasing use of media for sustainable development come questions relating to the ability of these channels to move beyond a one-way flow of information to include and respond to local knowledge and experiences and to create dialogue, both farmer to farmer and between farmers and designers of educational messaging. This article evaluates the role of media in promoting sustainable agriculture in Zambia. Specifically, the findings present qualitative feedback from 34 smallholder farmers targeted by Community Markets for Conservation's current radio programming efforts around sustainable agriculture. Results demonstrate the centrality of the radio program alongside other forms of communication, such as extension and farmer-to-farmer communication, as well as written and visual communication. These findings consider direct and indirect exposure to these

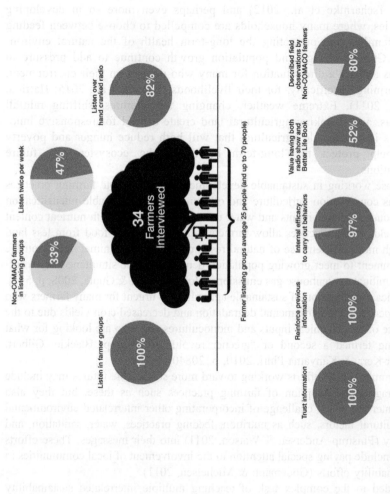

FIGURE 1 Social learning through direct and indirect exposure.
Note. Figure by Charles Floyd Design and Illustration (www.charlesfloyddesignandillustration.com).

efforts and the importance of radio in offering a foundation for dialogue and increased social diffusion of sustainable innovations in remote regions.

INTRODUCTION

Food security and biodiversity often are inextricably linked (Habel et al., 2015; Tscharntke et al., 2012) and perhaps even more so in developing countries, where many households are compelled to choose between feeding their families and protecting the long-term health of the natural environment. Climate change and population growth continue to add pressure to what is already a dire situation for many who depend on their environment, and farming specifically, for their livelihoods (Brown et al., 2015; Hatfield et al., 2011). Extreme weather, changing temperatures, shifting rainfall patterns, and shrinking agricultural land create a need for responsive innovations in sustainable agriculture that will both reduce hunger and poverty and help protect the long-term health of the ecosystem for future generations.

Those working in sustainable development often promote farming practices such as conservation agriculture and other means of sustainable intensification that reduce chemical inputs and water use while increasing both nutrient content and yield. These practices allow farmers to "produce more food from less land through more efficient use of natural resources and with minimal impact on the environment to meet growing population demands" while simultaneously working to mitigate greenhouse gas emissions (Hobbs, Sayre, & Gupta, 2008, p. 543). In Africa, the adoption of sustainable agriculture is urgent for many farmers who are experiencing environmental degradation and decreased crop yields due to the overuse of agrochemical inputs and monocultures and who are looking for what is being termed a second or "greener revolution" (Snapp, Blackie, Gilbert, Bezner-Kerr, & Kanyama-Phiri, 2010, p. 20840).

Communication efforts working toward more sustainable futures may include encouraging the adoption of farming practices such as these, but they also encounter the added challenge of incorporating other interrelated environmental and cultural factors, such as nutrition, feeding practices, water, sanitation, and poverty (Pinstrup-Andersen & Watson, 2011) into their messages. These efforts often include paying special attention to the involvement of local communities in sustainability efforts (Godemann & Michelsen, 2011).

Added to the complex task of teaching multiple interrelated sustainability issues in a way that involves local community members are the many challenges faced by those who seek to reach a broader audience with this information. As noted many times over, numerous sociocultural factors play a role in the acceptance, uptake, diffusion, and sustainability of innovations (Rogers, 2003). These factors might include perceptions, cultural norms, politics, and other preferences, and they are often interlinked, making understanding and responding to them a complex undertaking.

Although there is little substitution for the effectiveness of direct, interpersonal communication, many development initiatives involve use of media such as television, radio, and mobile phones because of their ability to reach large audiences with timely, relatively low-cost, and often entertaining information that has the potential to spark dialogue and change at both the individual and societal level. Less is known, however, about the impact of such campaigns focused on the complex task of sustainable development (Godemann & Michelsen, 2011; Mefalopulos & Grenna, 2004; Melkote, 2012; Moemeka, 1994; Quebral, 2012).

This article offers an evaluation of one organization's use of media to increase the adoption of sustainability agriculture among farmers in Zambia. Specifically, we examine audience responses to a specific radio program, *Farm Talk*, produced by Community Markets for Conservation (COMACO) and aired twice weekly throughout Zambia's Eastern Province. Further, we examine how *Farm Talk* enhances the uptake of information from another publication, *The Better Life Book*, and spurs dialogue among regional farmers. By applying a theory-based framework that highlights the importance of direct and indirect exposure, as well as identifying key variables for future analysis, the study's findings expand understanding of communication theory and campaign evaluation techniques in sustainable development contexts, such as rural Africa. The study also underscores some of the strengths and limitations of radio, especially as it interacts with print, extension, and farmer-to-farmer communication in facilitating the increased diffusion of sustainable innovations.

CASE STUDY: COMACO'S RADIO SHOW, *FARM TALK*

Founded by wildlife biologist Dale Lewis, COMACO began as a pilot program in 2003 and became a limited-by-guarantee company in 2009. Often used by nonprofits, a limited-by-guarantee company is focused more on advancing the aims of the company rather than profiting shareholders. As noted on the company's website, COMACO works to improve human health and conserve wildlife in Zambia by encouraging hunters to surrender their guns and snares and take up conservation agriculture as an alternative method of feeding their families and generating household income. The company also seeks to improve the agricultural yield, food security, health, and household income of existing farmers through increased soil and ecosystem health and the improved yields that often come with practicing conservation agriculture. COMACO currently has an estimated 140,000 farmer members using its conservation agriculture practices.

COMACO's educational efforts also include information on health and nutrition, sanitation, family planning, animal husbandry, beekeeping, wildlife conservation, and market strategy. The company offers premium market prices to members and maintains a popular product line in Zambia called "It's Wild!" that includes ingredients grown by COMACO farmers.

COMACO works at three primary levels: (a) household, (b) village chief/ headman, and (c) community. The company's organizational structure includes a local district government advisory committee, COMACO coordinators, area managers and extension workers, lead farmers, and farmer groups. Village farmer groups, organized by lead farmers, typically include around 15 farmers. Lead farmers (approximately 1,200), who are selected and trained by COMACO extension workers (approximately 90), are the first line of communication for village farmers. When lead farmers are unable to answer questions, village farmers turn to the extension workers who have been trained by COMACO staff. Both extension workers and lead farmers are encouraged to carry out the practices they teach. This enables them to experience firsthand some of the successes and challenges of applying innovations, strengthening their demonstration of techniques and outcomes to other farmers for improved understanding and trust.

COMACO's radio show, *Farm Talk*, began airing in the fall of 2013 as a way to enhance the organization's educational efforts and broaden its audience reach. The show offers COMACO a relatively low-cost method of reaching farmer members with timely reminders and additional information; it also allows the organization to reach a much wider audience of both members and nonmembers than it could without the use of media. The show, which initially lasted 30 minutes but was recently increased to 1 hour, airs on Wednesdays and Fridays each week around midday and has an estimated 200,000 listeners. *Farm Talk* is aired by Radio Breeze, which operates 24 hours a day with community-based, commercial, and public interest programming. The station's signal extends to the Eastern Province of Zambia, as well as to the Central and Northern parts of the country and Malawi and Mozambique, with a total possible listenership of around 1 million. In 2014, Walmart International donated 1,000 hand-cranked radios to COMACO to help support the *Farm Talk* radio show among farmers who otherwise might face challenges accessing electricity and purchasing batteries.

Farm Talk is aired in the language of Nyanja, considered a universal dialect in the Eastern Province of Zambia, where the majority of its listeners reside. The content is the same on Wednesday and Friday each week, giving farmers who cannot listen on one day a chance to hear the show another day, and giving them the opportunity to listen to more complex content twice to improve their understanding and recall. The show is produced by Filius Jere, who describes himself as an "old farmer broadcaster" (personal communication, 2014). The program includes information on a variety of topics relating to sustainability, including conservation agriculture and soil health (compost, tillage, agroforestry, crop rotation, fallow cropping, crop variety, basins, and mulching, among other things); information on poultry raising, beekeeping, health, and family planning; and important announcements on market information, technologies, or ways communities can partner with COMACO to earn good prices for their farm commodities.

Farm Talk follows a magazine format—typically opening with local music and singing, followed by an introduction to the overarching goal and topic of the episode. Content is interspersed with songs about the topic, followed by an entertaining "Come with me ..." segment, in which Jere travels out to a village to have local farmers share their personal stories and experiences. The show concludes with a summary and brief repeat of the singing played at the show's beginning. *Farm Talk* might be considered an innovative form of entertainment-education, a genre that combines entertainment and education to expose audience members to information intended to help create positive social change (Singhal, Cody, Rogers, & Sabido, 2004; Singhal & Rogers, 1999).

To complement the radio programming, COMACO also distributes *The Better Life Book*, a laminated print publication given to all lead farmers that includes technical information on most of the topics covered on *Farm Talk* through the use of heavily illustrated text. The book is created so that pages can be removed, updated, and added.

THEORETICAL FRAMEWORK

Hornik and Yanovitzky (2003) provided a framework for the evaluation of communication campaigns and, in this case, COMACO's efforts to increase the adoption of sustainable agriculture among farmers. Their framework is particularly useful because of its emphasis on both direct and indirect exposure to campaign messages, including individual-level exposure, beliefs and attitudes, self-efficacy, external constraints, and social norms and behaviors around the acceptance and diffusion of information. These elements, described in greater detail next, are brought to bear on understanding the role of media, and particularly *Farm Talk*, in the promotion of social learning about agriculture innovations in Zambia.

Direct Exposure

Communication campaigns intended to help spread an innovation are thought to have at least three pathways of influence: (a) direct exposure of individuals to the campaign messages, whether through media or some other communication channel; (b) direct exposure to messages created by other institutions based on the campaign themes, and (c) indirect exposure to campaign information from social diffusion (Hornik & Yanovitzky, 2003). This article focuses on the first and third of these pathways. The first of these, direct exposure of individuals to campaign messages, can come in a variety of forms, including interpersonal contact, campaign programs, written material, and mediated content. For COMACO farmers, this exposure presumably comes through interpersonal interactions with extension workers, the *Farm Talk* radio program, and the written and visual text of *The Better Life Book*.

Direct exposure typically allows people to learn about some of the costs and benefits that may come with adopting a particular behavior, including the time and money required or potential financial or social gains. This pathway of effects is perhaps the most common focus of campaign evaluations, and it draws from a number of key theories of health behavior change, including the theory of reasoned action (Fishbein & Ajzen, 1975, 2010) theory of planned behavior (Ajzen, 1985, 1988), health belief model (Becker, 1974; Rosenstock, 1990), and social cognitive theory (Bandura, 1986, 1997, 2001).

The theory of reasoned action and the theory of planned behavior take into consideration attitudes and beliefs that an individual has about a behavior, as well as perceived social norms and evaluations of potential outcomes in relation to intentions to perform the behavior (Ajzen, 1985, 1988; Fishbein & Ajzen, 1975, 2010). In the case of COMACO, for example, social norms related to media consumption may influence the uptake of information either by reinforcing or discouraging listening and adoption behaviors. In addition to social norms, Ajzen (2002) discussed the importance of considering both internal (self-efficacy) and external factors when considering how individuals might evaluate potential outcomes. Also, these concepts are taken up by Bandura (1997), who noted that challenges in innovation adoption may arise from not only an individual's sense of self-efficacy, meaning the individual's belief in his or her ability to plan and carry out a behavior, but also external factors beyond individual control, such as the weather or climate change in the case of agriculture.

Expanding further on these concepts, social cognitive theory (Bandura, 1986, 1997, 2001) pays special attention to the dynamic social and environmental context in which a behavior is learned and experienced, including factors leading to not only the adoption but also the maintenance of a behavior. Past experiences, which help form future expectations about the consequences of a behavior, are considered alongside internal and external reinforcements of the behavior, which themselves might be positive or negative. Observational learning also is an important component of social cognitive theory and an element of exposure that relates to indirect exposure of campaign messages.

Indirect Exposure

Campaign evaluations that focus on the individual level of exposure and its effects may miss other indirect but highly influential pathways (Hornik &

Yanovitzky, 2003). In fact, researchers have found that direct exposure, in some cases, has less influence on individual beliefs than indirect exposure (Yanovitzky, 2002). Often, social diffusion—interactions with family, friends, and others in the community—is a central route to the formation of attitudes and beliefs around a behavior.

Scholars have suggested that such diffusion might happen in two primary ways relating to dialogue—through the sharing of campaign information with those who were not exposed to the message themselves, or through the sparking of dialogue around the campaign innovation as those who were exposed discuss and ask and answer questions around the behavior (Yanovitzky & Stryker, 2001). Increasing dialogue and participation, both among campaign designers and farmers and from farmer to farmer, has the potential benefit of increasing the effectiveness of campaigns (Moemeka, 2000), as well as the long-term retention of campaign information. Finally, social diffusion also might occur through observational learning, which includes observing a model carrying out a behavior and the subsequent consequences (Bandura, 1986, 1997, 2001).

Also related to indirect effects of campaign exposure, social learning theory (Bandura, 2001) describes the socially mediated pathway as one in which media help connect audience members to networks and settings that have the potential to further motivate change. The interconnectedness of participants presents pathways for the diffusion of information, with sociocognitive factors impacting the selection of information that gets spread among these different pathways. Scholars of entertainment education often focus on the importance of catalyzing community dialogue, as well as dialogue among audience members, researchers, and program designers. Such dialogue has the potential to lead to greater equity through the increased sharing of information (Storey & Sood, 2013). Programming may directly encourage dialogue or create dialogue in more indirect but highly effective ways. In relation to community dialogue around a message, the size and stability of an individual's social network and the strength or weakness of ties often will influence whether a message is diffused in a way that increases the likelihood of adoption (Rice, 1993).

In sum, previous research underscores the role of social norms, efficacy, and direct and indirect exposure on the effectiveness of communication campaign efforts. Although such research has identified these factors in several contexts, most notably health, less research has examined it in relation to sustainable development or, more specifically, sustainable agriculture. We believe this poses an opportunity to explore these factors in a new and compelling context, extending previous work and offering new insights. Given the novel setting and exploratory nature of this work, rather than posing hypotheses, we ask the following research questions: What are the social norms around farmer listening to *Farm Talk*? How does indirect exposure to *Farm Talk* influence dialogue generation and observational learning among farmers around sustainable agriculture? How do *Farm Talk* and other communication efforts from COMACO impact farmers' learning about sustainable agriculture and adoption of new farming techniques?

METHODS

Interviews: Zambia's Eastern Province

We completed 34 in-depth interviews and one group interview with 30 small-scale farmers from villages in the areas of Mfuwe and Lundazi in the Eastern Province of Zambia in January 2014. We chose interviews over structured surveys, given the exploratory nature of this work. Questions enabled us to gather information about demographics, exposure, perceptions, comprehension, beliefs and attitudes, and adoption and diffusion. Questions were designed to help increase understanding of both direct and indirect pathways through which the radio program might be influencing farmers' beliefs, attitudes, and behaviors. The interview protocol, which received Institutional Board approval from the authors' university, appears in the appendix.

The challenges associated with conducting research in rural sub-Saharan Africa necessitated a close collaboration with COMACO in the implementation of the evaluation. The relationship with COMACO was established through the organization's partnership with Cornell's Atkinson Center for a Sustainable Future. We selected individual villages based on the presence of COMACO lead farmers and members. COMACO area managers suggested the villages where interviews took place, with the exception of one village that was visited spontaneously and another in which farmers had learned of the research and requested a visit.

We chose the regions of Mfuwe and Lundazi because of COMACO's presence there, with both central offices and community trading centers in each area, and because they represent different social and agricultural landscapes. Mfuwe, which borders South Luangwa National Park, has a long tradition of hunting. The farmers in this area are relatively new to agriculture; added to this challenge is a landscape that has suffered from severe drought in the past several years. Raising livestock is difficult for farmers living on or near the park because of predation. Historically, Lundazi is a farming region located on a plateau that gets significantly more rainfall than Mfuwe. Although predation is an issue in Lundazi, the region's distance from a gaming park greatly lowers the number of incidences. We sought to strengthen the quality of our findings and conclusions about the role of media in this context by interviewing farmers from these two regions.

Farmer responses were corroborated by field observations and responses among interviewees living and farming in the same village area.

Because of our primary focus on exploring the impacts of the radio program, added to time and resource constraints, we chose to interview for this study only COMACO farmers who listen to *Farm Talk* regularly. Prior to our arrival, extension workers notified farmers, and in most cases farmers came a few at a time from the fields for the interview. The village that was visited spontaneously was the exception; here, a group of around 30 female farmers came in from the field to participate in a discussion. Among the 34 individual farmers interviewed were four COMACO lead farmers. Half of the individual interviewees were female, except for the group interview, which had all female participants. The average age of interviewees was 33, with the youngest 29 and oldest 70. The average household size was seven, with the smallest having four members and the largest 16. Interviewees' average farm size was approximately 2 hectares, with farms ranging from .25 hectares to 7.5 hectares. Crops grown by those interviewed included maize, groundnuts, cotton, soybeans, sunflower, rice, soy, cassava, and sweet potato. Farmers were assured that their responses would never be linked to their names in resulting publications.

With the exception of the group interview, all interviews were conducted individually, lasting approximately 1 hour. The group discussion included only select interview questions. Due to more than 40 languages spoken in Zambia and multiple languages spoken in the regions where the interviews were conducted, we did not translate questions beforehand; instead, regional COMACO staff members acted as translators during the interviews.

We transcribed and imported the interviews into Atlas.ti for coding and analysis. Codes were both preestablished, based on the theoretical constructs just described, and developed as themes emerged from the data. Analysis focused on social learning through direct exposure, such as listening habits, comprehension, perceptions, preferences, trust, efficacy, and challenges associated with adoption. Measures explored the nature of exposure to *Farm Talk*, including how often farmers listen, where they listen, who they listen with, whether they comprehend the information presented, their perceptions of the purpose and benefits of the show, whether they trust COMACO and people on the show, and their perceptions of internal and external efficacy around implementing the innovations taught on the show. Codes that related to social learning through indirect exposure included dialogue generated immediately before and after the program airs each week, as well as "dialogue" between the various campaign communication channels, including the radio program, *The Better Life Book*, extension workers, and farmer-to-farmer dialogue at home and in the fields.

RESULTS

Social Learning via Direct Exposure

Frequency. Figure 1 provides a summary of the results. As noted earlier, *Farm Talk* airs the same program twice each week, on Wednesdays at 2:30 p.m. and on Fridays at 11:30 a.m. Forty-seven percent of the farmers interviewed reported listening to the program on both days. Of the farmers who listened once a week, one said that the lead farmer divided his two farmer groups so that one listened on Wednesday and one on Friday. Others explained that the later time on Wednesday worked well because the show airs at about the time they usually come in from the fields, but they had to miss Friday's show because they were still working during that time. Others said they simply did not listen a second time because the show was a repeat. Of those who do listen twice a week, farmers said they enjoyed listening twice because it reminded them of what to do and helped them remember the information. One farmer said that if he missed pieces of information when listening on Wednesday, those gaps could be filled by listening again on Friday. Farmers said radio reception was good but occasionally interrupted by power outages.

Accessibility. Nearly all of the farmers interviewed reported using the hand-cranked radios most of the time when listening to the show; 82% said they always used the hand-cranked radios, 12% said they usually use the radios, and only 6% said they do not use the radios. Farmers who usually, but not always, used the hand-cranked radios said that they use these radios only when the lead farmer is present and otherwise use their own radios. The two farmers who reported not using the hand-cranked radios said that they were not provided with radios. Farmers described the radios as easy to crank, but many farmers found it necessary to also use small solar panels to keep the radios powered for the show's duration. Farmers said that challenges arose when there was inadequate sun. We also observed that in one instance, cranking the radio kept it powered only for about 15 minutes, or half of the show, causing it to cut off during an important segment while farmers spent time recranking it.

Social Norms Related to Listening. Almost all farmers reported listening to *Farm Talk* with their COMACO farmer group. The exceptions were one farmer who reported listening with his family, one who listened with a group of students in town, and one who said he listens with his neighbor on days when the show is on and the group does not meet. Almost half of the farmers said that their groups gather to listen under a tree, with some describing elevating the radio in the middle of the group on a table or hanging from a pole for better volume and reception. About 35% said they meet at the lead farmer's house to listen; another farmer said his group meets in the center of town to listen.

The listening groups ranged in size from eight to 70 people, with an average of 25. Of the interviewees, 15 said that non-COMACO farmers regularly join their group to listen to *Farm Talk*; of these groups, non-COMACO farmers make up an average of 33% of the audience. One farmer said that he has observed some non-COMACO farmers who listened to the show adopting new farming methods and using COMACO's guidelines. The farmer who reported listening to the show with a group of seven students in town said that because he was the only COMACO farmer, the students looked to him to answer questions after the show each week.

Language Challenges. When asked if they had any challenges with the language used on the show (Nyanja/Chewa) or if they would prefer a different language, all farmers said they could understand the language. Farmers in Lundazi, however, overwhelmingly said they would like to see the language of Tumbuka represented on the show, with one farmer saying, "This is Tumbuka land—if programs could be in Tumbuka it would be very effective; yes, we understand Chewa but there are some terms that take time to understand."

Comprehension and Recall. When farmers were asked if the show presents information at a pace that allows them to follow and remember what they are learning, all answered that it did, except for one farmer who said that occasionally presenters speak too quickly. One group of farmers has appointed a secretary, who takes notes in case something is missed; others said that they discuss the information and get clarification from the lead farmer. Two farmers said the show was presented in a way that was detailed and easy to follow, allowing them to implement what they have heard. One farmer said, "The program is not only helping COMACO but others as well because it's educational but simplified, and even those who are not yet COMACO farmers have gained a desire to practice." Another similarly stated,

> There are two sets of people in the group—one already taught, and one being newly recruited learning new things, and the program is simplified and the quality of the lessons are such that the newly recruited can also understand; but it is the duty of lead farmers to make appointments to visit in person.

Trust and Reinforcement. When asked if they trusted the information learned on the show, every interviewee said yes. One farmer added that although they trust the information, they still will consult with the area extension worker to get his views before applying what is learned. Another said they trust the information because "what is said, we have seen." Several others said that they trust the information on the show because they have tried it, and it works. One farmer said that farmers trust the information on the radio because it is the same as what they have learned from the extension workers. Another farmer attributed his trust in the show to the confidence of those presenting. Others said they trust the show because they have heard a lot of success stories. One farmer said that the trust level for *Farm Talk* is much higher than for other radio programs.

When asked if they trusted the other farmers on the show, all but two of the interviewees answered yes. Of those answering yes, one said that she trusts what the farmers are saying despite not being able to see what they are doing firsthand. Another said she trusts the farmers on the show "because for someone to be interviewed and speaking from experience, they are speaking the truth;" another farmer said, "For that person to talk about what they're doing means they've seen the benefit." One interviewee acknowledged trusting the farmers on the show but added the following caveat: "I have to see if what they're saying is working to see if it's benefiting them first, then I will adopt it."

One of the farmers who said she did not trust the other farmers on the show explained that is difficult to trust peers or leaders from the community unless they come from a reputable organization, such as COMACO or the Ministry of Agriculture. When asked as a follow-up question relating to how this interviewee felt about private companies in the region, she said it was difficult to trust them because they want her to grow things like cotton, which she doesn't want to grow. She added that if they were talking about something she wanted to learn she might trust them more, but she prefers learning from COMACO and the Ministry of Agriculture.

Despite the extent of trust in the farmers on the show, when asked from whom they would prefer to learn new information (e.g., peers, lead farmers, their village chief, extension workers, or experts), none answered peers alone; most said they would prefer to learn new information from the extension workers and lead farmers, with about 30% saying they would be happy learning from any of these sources.

Knowledge Acquisition. All of the 34 individually interviewed farmers said that the radio show helps to remind them of information they had learned from extension workers or COMACO farmer field days. One farmer estimated that about three fourths of what is aired on *Farm Talk* already has been learned and is serving as affirmation. Others described the show as reinforcement, with one farmer saying they would most likely forget a lot of the information if it were not for the show. When considering the benefits of the show beyond offering reinforcement of previously learned lessons, farmers said that it helped remind them when to carry out certain activities relating to conservation agriculture, such as when to plant and when to apply compost. Along with timely farming information, one farmer said that the show also offers information about the market season. When talking about some of the additional benefits of the program, one farmer described the show as offering answers to some of the questions that come up, saying that there are times when she will go in the field to ask questions that she and other farmers are having a hard time answering, and the radio program often will answer these questions for them. This same farmer also described learning about the experiences of other farmers, saying that she "heard women (even single or widowed) in the plateau who have managed to have 300 bags of corn, 250 bags of groundnuts, Irish potatoes, sweet potatoes, cassava." She went on to explain that the show has helped her learn about the different techniques and experiences in the valley and the plateau, saying, "Here in valley we use the hoe; there they use ox drawn." She also described learning about new crop varieties on the show and said that the show serves the purpose of arousing interest in new techniques. Another farmer described how they "used to have small fields but through testimonies from COMACO, farmers in the plateau have expanded fields."

Others described building on their knowledge of conservation agriculture through the show. Several farmers described learning about illegal poaching and the benefits of wildlife conservation for the first time on the show, with one farmer describing,

> You can still have protein without killing wildlife but keeping chickens, cattle, pigs and goats; some years ago, farmers would go poaching and kill a lot of animals, but today they know how to keep livestock for protein. This was learned in combination from radio and from other farmers.

Efficacy and Perceptions of Behavioral Control. As a measure of internal efficacy, farmers were asked if they believed they had the skills to try new techniques and innovations presented on *Farm Talk*. In response, all but one said yes. One farmer said she tries new things with zeal. Another qualified his answer by saying that when he sees or hears something new, if it is well explained, he feels confident in trying it, but if it is not, he will have to learn more. When asked if they felt they had the resources to try new innovations, all of the farmers expressed the need for greater access to material resources, including hoes for gardening, local chicken feed, and materials for bee hives. Several farmers said lack of rainfall was an issue, and one farmer said that more reading materials were needed to have the instructions for digging basins and other activities.

Social Learning via Indirect Exposure

Indirect exposure to campaign messages occurs in several ways around *Farm Talk*. First, dialogue takes place before or after the program among farmers and often a farmer leader. Second, there is a kind of "dialogue" or reinforcement of messages that occurs between communication channels, with the radio show, the printed *Better Life Book*, and in-person training. Third, dialogue and observations occur in farmers' fields around campaign message implementation. To better understand information seeking and the diffusion and adoption of COMACO's innovations from farmer to farmer, we sought to understand behavior, historically and in the present, around the adoption of farming innovations, perceptions of risk in adopting new innovations, and the sharing of successes and failures.

Dialogue Before and After the Show. In relation to the dialogue that takes place just before or after the show, all farmers described sitting and listening quietly during the program and remaining afterward to discuss and ask questions from 15 minutes to 2 hours, with the average time spent talking afterward at 40 minutes. One farmer said that his group usually meets before the program starts, with the group coming as early as 10 a.m. for the 11:30 a.m. show to discuss issues and ask questions; he described this as their time to update each other. Farmers described asking questions of the lead farmers and sharing experiences with one another. When a lead farmer is unable to answer specific questions, they will contact the COMACO extension worker in their area by cell phone. Extension workers said that when they get calls from lead farmers with questions, they typically try to come to the village in person to answer them. Lead farmers also reported referring to *The Better Life Book* to help answer questions.

Dialogue between Communication Channels. Of the farmers interviewed, 31 were familiar with *The Better Life Book*, and of those, 52% said they value having both the radio program and the book; 32% said they prefer the radio to the book, and 16% said they prefer the book to the radio. Reasons given by farmers as to why they value both the radio and the book included being able to learn from the radio but refer to the book when the radio show was not airing; further, when there were questions during the week, the two formats supplement and complement each other. One farmer described the radio show as giving "prompt and swift information about new things," whereas the book reviews things that have been learned before. Another farmer said the information in both sources was the same, but the book helped if someone was stuck with a question. Others described the value of the radio show for those who are illiterate and can "only learn by hearing."

Those who prefer *Farm Talk* over *The Better Life Book* described the radio show as creating a platform for discussion and interaction. One farmer explained, "If you forgot you might hear the radio and be reminded, you might forget about the book." Others saw the radio as a source for learning when the lead farmer, who keeps the book, was not able to come visit them. Those who preferred the book over the radio described the radio program as limited with lessons that come and go, saying the [The Better Life Book] will always be with me." Another farmer responded by asking, "How do you remember directions like making compost that are quite detailed and technical? *Better Life Book*." One farmer described the pages as having information that has been "proven in the pictures," with another farmer saying similarly that the book includes "visible pictures, and the radio we just hear and can't prove."

The dialogue between *Farm Talk* and *The Better Life Book*, along with the dialogue between lead farmers and extension workers, appears to help the interviewees seek information and fill in gaps in their learning, with each channel serving a somewhat unique purpose. Beyond this form of dialogue, dialogue occurs from farmer to farmer away from the radio show, including those who are members of COMACO and those who have been exposed to campaign messages to different degrees.

Farmer-to-Farmer Dialogue. To better understand the ways in which innovations taught by COMACO are shared from farmer to farmer at the village level, we asked farmers if they and others in their village often tried new methods, if this was different from in the past, if they believed there was a lot of risk in trying new methods, if they typically shared their successes and failures with one another, and how others typically respond when they see someone trying something new.

When asked if farmers in their village often try new farming methods, all answered positively, with one saying that the radio has aroused interest in this village around new methods. Another farmer said that all groups of people could be found, some who really like change and others who "stick to their old methods," with some interested and some who do not want to learn new methods. When asked why he thought some people were more interested than others, this farmer said that they "differ in personality," with some being eager to try new things and others who "don't have the heart." Other farmers said that they were interested and willing to try new things and believed most farmers want to learn new things; others said that as long as resources permit, they were willing to try new things.

When asked if farmers had previously tried new farming methods, 71% said that they had, with nearly one fourth of those saying that the new methods did not work. Two farmers said that the information used was inaccurate, and another said that their soils had been depleted from chemical fertilizers. When asked if the experience had made it hard to trust the farming innovations taught by COMACO, one farmer said that they trusted COMACO because they have been working together for a while and COMACO extension and lead farmers come to their fields to help them with practical implementation.

When farmers were asked if they feel there is a lot of risk involved in trying new methods, most farmers expressed that there was risk involved but that it was worth the risk to try new innovations. One female farmer stated,

> Before COMACO, I was the type of person who would not try new things, I was too busy just trying to eat—trying to get a plate of mealie meal. I walked a long distance to the clinic with my children on my back because I had no money to pay for transportation.

This same farmer said that she now believed that "risk takers succeed. If you're afraid to take risks, you never go anywhere. We work hard to overcome challenges (feed for example) because we want to better our lives."

When asked if farmers share successes and failures in trying new methods with other farmers, most farmers said yes, with one saying,

> We do question one another when we try something and it doesn't work. For example, compost manure—if it doesn't work we'll talk together to find out why it's working for one and not for another.

Others said that they share to learn and encourage one another. In one farmer group, the lead farmer has the group gather once a month to share successes and failures, and then he conducts field visits to verify what farmers have reported. Others said that they share successes and failures, comparing yields, suggesting interventions, and contacting the extension worker if they are stuck on an issue. Another said that farmer successes and failures become the main topic when they are chatting with friends and family.

Observational Learning. When asked how they and others respond when they see someone trying something new, most of the farmers said that when they try something new themselves, others will come to learn more from them. When this interaction between farmers occurs in the fields, it takes several forms. Approximately 80% of farmers described others coming to their fields to observe what they were doing. Of these, over one fourth of the farmers said that those who come to observe would tease, taunting and saying the methods won't work. One farmer said that he ignored the teasing and that the teasing often happened until the person observing saw that the method worked; he added that farmers in his village would not sabotage one another's efforts. Another said that there was teasing until she was able to explain the reason for what she was doing, and another said that farmers would mock and laugh, but he would tell them, "Just wait." Others said that peers were very open and "anxious" to learn new ideas, and would admire them for trying new methods and ask questions about the benefits.

DISCUSSION AND CONCLUSIONS

This evaluation of COMACO's *Farm Talk* examines the role of media and its interaction with other communication channels, such as the printed *The Better Life Book* and interpersonal communication, in efforts to enhance sustainable development in Zambia. The research provided insight into the social norms around listening to the radio program, including how often farmers listen, where they listen, and with whom they listen to the show. It also examined farmers' comprehension of the information on the show, perceptions of the show's purpose and benefits, perceptions of internal efficacy and behavioral control around implementing the innovations taught on the show, and trust in the sources of information (here, COMACO and others on the show). It also investigated some of the ways that *Farm Talk* and other communication efforts from COMACO, particularly *The Better Life Book*, are generating dialogue and observational learning and influencing farmers' attitudes and beliefs related to sustainable agriculture. Finally, it highlighted some challenges associated with language and the use of the hand-cranked radios.

Hornik and Yanovitzky's (2003) framework for campaign evaluation helped us highlight the ways in which social learning, facilitated by direct and indirect exposure to COMACO's messages, plays an important role in the adoption of sustainable innovations in the development context. In relation to direct exposure, the results showed that many farmers benefit from repeated exposure to campaign information, with nearly half of those interviewed listening to the same *Farm Talk* content twice a week. It also showed that farmers listen to the program in group settings that include both COMACO and non-COMACO farmers and that COMACO farmers believe that the amount of information and detail is easy to comprehend for both of these groups. This evaluation underscores the role that radio can play in offering timely agricultural information, as well as its important role in reinforcing campaign messages through complementary channels.

With regard to indirect exposure, the results suggest that *Farm Talk* helps generate dialogue among farmers about the show's content before and after the show and in the village and the fields. It also showed an important interaction between the radio show, extension workers, farmer-to-farmer communication, and *The Better Life Book*, with each channel playing a unique and often complementary role.

Finally, results show that many farmers are eager to learn and practice sustainable farming techniques despite the real and perceived risk of adopting them. Such risks range from inclement and unpredictable weather, to ineffective or insufficient tools, to social factors such as taunting or teasing by neighbors. One explanation for this finding may be the trust that farmers placed in COMACO and its extension workers and peer-to-peer networks.

Although such trust does not come without careful cultivation, this finding underscores the importance of the messenger in the uptake of information. The influence of social learning (Bandura, 1997) also played a clear role in that "seeing is believing" was a frequent explanation for adoption of sustainable agriculture.

Given the importance of social learning and reinforcement to the success of campaigns, future research might explore more participatory features in communication efforts. All of the farmers interviewed said that they would like to see drama added to the show, and many expressing an interest in participating in drama creation for the show. Many said that they would appreciate a "call in" or text feature that would allow them to ask questions or request more information. Exploring the use of drama as a way to illustrate the interconnected nature of human and environmental health may be a way to enhance self-efficacy while linking sustainability issues relating to soil health, agroecology, climate change, and human health and nutrition in a way that is both informative and engaging for farmers. Adding a call-in or text feature also has the potential to enhance farmer learning, as well as strengthening campaign message development through community participation, among other things.

Alongside the findings, it is important to point out study limitations. These include the sample, which comprised a self-selected audience of *Farm Talk* radio listeners who were also COMACO members. It is possible that farmers were biased by their relationship with COMACO and less willing to provide negative feedback on the program. Further, although some interviewees commented on their perceptions of the adoption of COMACO methods by nonmembers or nonlisteners of the program, these secondhand accounts must be viewed with caution. Future studies should assess more systemically the impact of *Farm Talk* on listeners in comparison with non-listeners. In addition, although in-depth interviews provided the ability to explore in greater detail the meanings and interpretations farmers ascribed to *Farm Talk* and *The Better Life Book*, they cannot provide the generalizability of findings deemed valuable in much evaluation research. A large-scale survey would enable measurement of key variables noted in the literature that play important roles in a campaign's effectiveness. Future research should seek to ascertain whether the findings observed in this case study are generalizable to a wider sample using random selection sampling procedures and methods that can produce generalizable results. Finally, although we did include farmers from two different regions, the study was not designed to ascertain whether regional differences influenced the adoption of COMACO's farming innovations. Future research should examine whether some of the practical and even cultural differences lead to different degrees of willingness to adopt sustainable farming recommendations.

Despite its limitations, this study offers an important benchmark in assessing farmers' responses to *Farm Talk* and support for those charged with enhancing sustainable development to better understand some of the complex considerations of designing and implementing campaigns. In doing so, it adds to our understanding of the value and importance of theory-based evaluations that consider both direct and indirect exposure pathways to social learning about sustainability. Although most evaluations focus on direct effects, these results show that indirect effects can be just as impactful, and often more so. Further, at a time when new media technologies seem to dominate campaign efforts, this study also underscores the importance of examining more traditional media—in this case, radio and books—which still play important roles in regions that have little access to electricity, much less wireless networking. Even so, with an expected increase in access to mobile technologies, such as mobile phones, future research should examine ways to enhance current communication efforts with new technologies as they become more widely adopted in Zambia.

ACKNOWLEDGMENTS

This project was funded by the David R. Atkinson Center for a Sustainable Future (ACSF) at Cornell University. Individuals who helped with the fieldwork but not the content of this article include Alexander Travis, Cornell University; Dale Lewis, president and founder of COMACO; and Filius Jere, journalist, farmer, and producer of *Farm Talk*. Exemption from Institutional Review Board review has been approved according to Cornell IRB Policy #2 and under paragraph 2 of the Department of Health and Human Services Code of Federal Regulations 45CFR 46.101(b).

REFERENCES

Ajzen, I. (1985). From intentions to actions: A theory of planned behavior. In J. Kuhl, & J. Beckmann (Eds.), *Action-control: From cognitions to behavior* (pp. 11–39). New York, NY: Springer-Verlag.

Ajzen, I. (1988). *Attitudes, personality, and behavior.* Chicago, IL: Dorsey.

Ajzen, I. (2002). Perceived behavioral control, self-efficacy, locus of control, and the theory of planned behavior. *Journal of Applied Social Psychology, 32,* 665–683.

Bandura, A. (1986). *The social foundation of thought and action: A social cognitive theory.* Englewood Cliffs, NJ: Prentice-Hall.

Bandura, A. (1997). *Self-efficacy: The exercise of control.* New York, NY: Freeman.

Bandura, A. (2001). Social cognitive theory of mass communication. *Media Psychology, 3,* 265–299.

Becker, M. H. (Ed.). (1974). *The health belief model and personal health behavior.* Thorofare, NJ: Charles B. Slack.

CLIMATE AND SUSTAINABILITY COMMUNICATION

Brown, M. E., Antle, J. M., Backlund, P., Carr, E. R., Easterling, W. E., Walsh, M. K., ... Tebaldi, C. (2015). *Climate change, global food security, and the U.S. food system.* Washington, DC: U.S. Global Change Research Program.

Fishbein, M., & Ajzen, I. (1975). *Belief, attitude, intention and behavior: An introduction to theory and research.* Reading, MA: Addison-Wesley.

Fishbein, M., & Ajzen, I. (2010). *Predicting and changing behavior: The reasoned action approach.* New York, NY: Taylor & Francis.

Godemann, J., & Michelsen, G. (Eds.). (2011). *Sustainability communication.* Dordrecht, the Netherlands: Springer Netherlands.

Habel, J. C., Teucher, M., Hornetz, B., Jaetzold, R., Kimatu, J. N., Kasili, S., ... Len, L. (2015). Real-world complexity of food security and biodiversity conservation. *Biodiversity and Conservation, 24*(6), 1531–1539.

Hatfield, J. L., Boote, K. J., Kimball, B. A., Ziska, L. H., Izaurralde, R. C., Ort, D., ... Wolfe, D. (2011). Climate impacts on agriculture: Implications for crop production. *Agronomy Journal, 103,* 351–370.

Hobbs, P. R., Sayre, K., & Gupta, R. (2008). The role of conservation agriculture in sustainable agriculture. *Philosophical Transactions of the Royal Society of London B: Biological Sciences, 363* (149), 1543–1555.

Hornik, R., & Yanovitzky, I. (2003). Using theory to design evaluations of communication campaigns: The case of the national youth anti-drug media Campaign. *Communication Theory, 13*(2), 204–224.

Mefalopulos, P., & Grenna, L. (2004). Promoting sustainable development through strategic communication. In D. Hamu, E. Auchincloss, & W. Goldstein (Eds.), *Communicating protected areas* (pp. 24–31). Gland, Switzerland: IUCN Commission on Education and Communication.

Melkote, S. (2012). *Development communication in directed social change: A reappraisal of theory and practice.* Singapore: Asian Media Information and Communication Centre.

Moemeka, A. A. (2000). *Development Communication in Action: Building Understanding and Creating Participation.* The Rowman & Littlefield Publishing Group (formerly known as University Press of America), Blue Ridge Summit, PA.

Moemeka, A. A. (1994). *Communicating for development: A new pan-disciplinary perspective.* Albany: SUNY Press.

Pinstrup-Andersen, P., & Watson, D. (2011). *Food policy in developing countries: The role of government in global, national, and local food systems.* Ithaca, NY: Cornell University Press.

Quebral, N. C. (2012). The underside of communication in development. *NORDICOM Review: Nordic Research on Media and Communication, 33,* 59.

Rice, R. E. (1993). Using network concepts to clarify sources and mechanisms of social influence. In W. Richards, Jr., & G. Barnett (Eds.), *Progress in communication sciences, Vol. 12: Advances in communication network analysis* (pp. 43–52). Norwood, NJ: Ablex.

Rogers, E. M. (2003). *Diffusion of innovations.* New York, NY: Free Press.

Rosenstock, I. M. (1990). The health belief model: Explaining health behavior through expectancies. In K. Glanz, F. M. Lewis, & B. K. Rimer (Eds.), *Health behavior and health education* (pp. 39–62). San Francisco, CA: Jossey-Bass.

Singhal, A., Cody, M. J., Rogers, E. M., & Sabido, M. (Eds.). (2004). *Entertainment-Education and social change: History, research, and practice.* Mahwah, NJ: Erlbaum.

Singhal, A., & Rogers, E. M. (1999). *Entertainment-education: A communication strategy for social change.* Mahwah, NJ: Erlbaum.

Snapp, S. S., Blackie, M. J., Gilbert, R. A., Bezner-Kerr, R., & Kanyama-Phiri, G. Y. (2010). Biodiversity can support a greener revolution in Africa. *Proceedings of the National Academy of Sciences, 107*(48), 20840–20845.

Storey, D., & Sood, S. (2013). Increasing equity, affirming the power of narrative and expanding dialogue: The evolution of entertainment education over two decades. *Critical Arts: South-North Cultural and Media Studies*, 27(1), 9–35.

Tscharntke, T., Clough, Y., Wanger, T. C., Jackson, L., Motzke, I., Perfecto, I., ... Whitbread, A. (2012). Global food security, biodiversity conservation and the future of agricultural intensification. *Biological Conservation*, 151, 53–59.

Yanovitzky, I. (2002). Effect of news coverage on the prevalence of drunk-driving behavior: Evidence from a longitudinal study. *Journal of Studies on Alcohol*, 63, 342–351.

Yanovitzky, I., & Stryker, J. (2001). Mass media, social norms, and health promotion efforts: A longitudinal study of media effects on youth binge drinking. *Communication Research*, 28, 208–239.

APPENDIX
COMACO's Radio Communication Efforts in Zambia

Farm Talk Farmer Interview
Demographics
Name
Village
Approximate age
Household size
Size of farm (lima)

Exposure (to *Farm Talk*, COMACO, and information from other sources)

How did you learn about *Farm Talk*?
When did you begin listening to the show?
How often do you listen?
What days/times?
Do you have any conflicts with the time of the show?
How do you listen?
Where do you usually listen?
Who are you usually with? [For Farmer Leaders: Ask how they determine which group they listen with, how many usually come, and if/how they keep track of who is there]
Do you sit down and listen, or do other things while the show is on?
Do you talk about the show with others while it is airing?
Do you talk about the show after listening? If so, with who typically?
Do you typically use the hand-cranked radio provided by COMACO or another radio to listen?
Do you have any challenges with the hand-cranked radio or your other radio (use, reception)?
Do you have any challenges with the language used in the show?

Would you prefer the show to be in a different language?
Have you ever worked with one of COMACO's extension workers?
If so, who?
When?
For how long?
What work did you do together /what did you learn?
Did you use what you learned from them? Do you still use the information?
Are you familiar with the product line called "It's Wild!"?
Have you ever sold crops to COMACO? Why or why not?
Do you sell to other buyers?

Perceptions, Comprehension, and Recall
Who do you think is the target audience for *Farm Talk*?
Do you trust the information on the show?
Do you trust the farmers on the show?
Would you prefer to learn new information from peers, lead farmers, chief, extension workers, experts?
Do you care about the characters and look forward to hearing the next show?
Who is your favorite character?
Who is your least favorite character?
Do you like the format of the show? Why or why not? (entertaining? boring? same story repeated?)
The show is in a "magazine format" with talk, expert presenter, farmer presenter; would you prefer a different format?
How would you feel about having a call in show once a month?
How would you feel about adding drama to the show?
Is the program too long?
What do you like best about the show? Least? [anything you don't like]
Have you learned anything new from listening to the show? If so, what?
Have you learned anything about wildlife from listening to the show? If so, what?
Have you learned anything about farming from listening to the show? If so, what?
Have you used anything that you learned on the show? Is so, what?
Do you continue to use what you learned? Why or why not?
Has *Farm Talk* helped you remember things you learned from extension workers or field days?
What do you think is the purpose of the show?
Does the show go at a pace that allows you to follow and remember what you're hearing?
Is there too much information/detail?

Would you request more information if it were available? (via text or pamphlet)

Beliefs and Attitudes/Adoption and Diffusion

Do farmers in your village often try new farming methods (new ways of growing, inputs,crops, etc.)?

How do others respond when you or someone else tries something new?

When you learn something new, how do you decide whether to try it yourself? Talk with others? If so, who?

Wait for others to try it first? If so, who?

Do you feel you have the skills to try new farming methods successfully?

Do you feel your have the resources (access to materials, etc.) available to try new methods?

What are some of the challenges you face when trying new things?

How often have you tried new farming methods in the past?

Do you feel there is a lot of risk involved in trying new methods/risk involved in not trying new methods?

Do you and other farmers share with one another successes and failures in trying new methods?

General/Wrap-Up

Are you familiar with COMACO's *Better Life Book*?

Do you prefer to learn new information from the book or from the radio? Why?

What other topics would you like to learn about on the show?

Is there anything you would change about the show?

Do you have a mobile phone number or email you would like to share?

For Farmer Leaders: Would a feedback form that allowed you to report attendance and send comments and questions to COMACO be helpful?

"Maybe Yes, Maybe No?": Testing the Indirect Relationship of News Use through Ambivalence and Strength of Policy Position on Public Engagement with Climate Change

Jay D. Hmielowski

Edward R. Murrow College of Communication
Washington State University

Erik C. Nisbet

Department of Communication
Ohio State University

This article uses a national online survey to examine whether political ideology moderates the indirect relationship of conservative and nonconservative media use through intra-attitudinal consistency (i.e., ambivalence) and strength of policy position (i.e., how strongly people support or oppose mitigation policies) on intention to take political action regarding the issue of climate change. Results show that conservative media use increases intention to take political action through our two intervening variables among conservatives and moderates and decreases engagement through the same variables among liberals. Our results also showed similar findings in the opposite direction for nonconservative media.

Problems associated with climate change are looming on the horizon; rising temperatures are changing the environment in ways that threaten life on Earth (IPCC, 2013). Scholars have extensively examined how communication can affect attitudes toward climate change (for a review, see Moser, 2010). However, gaps exist in research regarding the influence of the media on the public's attitudes and whether people are willing to take action on mitigation policies. One such gap is the need to understand whether supportive or opposing information from media outlets increases or decreases the complexity of people's attitudes. There is also a need to understand how the complexity (or lack of complexity) of people's attitudes fits into larger communication processes focused on important outcome variables, such as how strongly people support or oppose mitigation policies and people's intention to take political action regarding those policies. This article addresses both of these issues.

A number of recent studies have reexamined the cross-pressures hypothesis to understand people's level of political engagement (i.e., their willingness to take action on an issue). Indeed, these studies have shown that hearing supportive information tends to increase engagement, whereas hearing opposing information tends to decrease levels of engagement (Dilliplane, 2011). More recently, scholars have tried to expand on this line of research by looking at what variables could explain why supportive (or opposing) information increases (or decreases) engagement (Wojcieszak, et al., 2016). In this study, we expand on these findings by including important dimensions of people's attitudes concerning environmental problems. Social scientists have started to expand on the conceptualization of attitudes by adding a second dimension to the existing unidimensional scale that focuses on whether people hold both positive and negative attitudes toward objects. This second dimension adds an assessment of attitudinal ambivalence, which is the extent to which people simultaneously hold opposing attitudes in their memory. Research examining ambivalence has shown that looking at this oft-ignored dimension of attitudes has important consequences for how people process information (Bromer, 1998), their use of heuristics when making decisions (Basinger & Lavine, 2005), information-seeking behaviors (Maio, Bell, & Esses, 1996), and levels of engagement (Castro, Garrido, Reis, & Menezes, 2009). In addition to ambivalence, we also include strength of policy support as an additional mediating variable.

This article contributes to the extant literature by examining the relationship between conservative and nonconservative news use on attitudinal ambivalence. Using data from a national online survey conducted in the spring of 2011, we examine whether political ideology moderates the relationship between conservative and nonconservative programing on ambivalence. We also examine how ambivalence fits into larger communication processes by including a measure of conflicting attitudes as a mediating variable in a serial mediation model. We posit that the relationship between conservative and nonconservative media use with intention to mobilize regarding climate change can be explained, in part, by the degree of ambivalence and strength of policy position. The inclusion of ambivalence allows for a more nuanced understanding of how the use of supportive (or opposing) information increases (or decreases) attitude complexity. Moreover, it shows the potentially important role that the complexity (or lack of complexity) of attitudes in understanding people's strength of policy position and their level of intention to mobilize with the issue of climate change.

CLIMATE CHANGE, PARTISAN MEDIA, AND ENGAGEMENT

In general, research has shown that the public is not taking action to address the issue of climate change (Leiserowitz, Maibach, Roser-Renouf, & Hmielowski, 2012). One variable that could be important relative to understanding why people do (or do not) take action on climate change is the information people hear about this issue through the media. A number of studies have highlighted the important role that different communication variables could have on understanding attitudes and engagement with the issue of climate change (for a review, see Moser, 2010). Scholars also have become interested in understanding the process of communicating environmental and science issues in politicized environments (Jamieson & Hardy, 2014; Lupia, 2013). In particular, they have started to examine the relationship between hearing divergent media messages on different outlets and attitudes about climate change.

A number of recent studies have shown relationships between coverage on outlets that report (and challenge) scientific consensus on climate and a range of outcomes. For instance, research has shown that hearing information that supports scientific consensus surrounding climate change (i.e., coverage on network news and liberal outlets) increases trust in scientists, beliefs that climate change is happening, and support for climate change mitigation policies (Feldman, Maibach, Roser-Renouf, & Leiserowitz, 2012; Feldman, Myers, Hmielowski, & Leiserowitz, 2014; Hmielowski, Feldman, Myers, Leiserowitz, & Maibach, 2014; Nisbet, Cooper, & Garrett, 2015). By contrast, media that question the validity of climate scientists (i.e., coverage on conservative outlets such as Fox News) tend to decrease levels of all of these variables (Feldman et al., 2014; Hmielowski et al., 2014). Because the political parties in the United States have shown divergent views on climate change (McCright & Dunlap, 2011), studies also have looked at the relationship between hearing supportive or opposing information from various outlets and beliefs about this issue. For instance, Feldman and her colleagues (2012) found that use of outlets that question scientific consensus (e.g., Fox News) was associated with greater disbelief of the existence of climate change among conservatives. Up to this point, these studies have yet to examine engagement with the issue of climate change. However, given that research has shown that hearing divergent information about climate change is related to various attitudinal outcomes, use of these outlets could be associated with intention to take political action on the issue of climate change. Moreover, research suggests that attitudes could serve an important role in predicting behavior (Ajzen, 2011), which means it is important for scholars to examine similar intervening variables between the use of media and engagement with this environmental issue.

THE CROSS-PRESSURES HYPOTHESIS

Media scholars have examined the relationship between media use and people's level of intention to engage in actions that would help the environment (Holbert, Kwak, & Shah, 2003). This line of inquiry has expanded in today's media system that provides people with greater choice over the content they choose to watch. Today, people have more opportunities to seek out supportive and opposing information via partisan TV (e.g., Fox News and MSNBC) and Internet outlets (e.g., Redstate.com and Huffington Post). This idea of the consistency or lack of consistency of information originates from early communication research focused on cross-pressures (Lazarsfeld, Berelson, & Gaudet, 1968). The cross-pressure hypothesis proposed that contradictory and opposing influences may be associated with decreased levels of political interest and delayed vote time decisions (Lazarsfeld et al., 1968).

Lazarsfeld's work on the cross-pressures hypothesis focused on internal factors that contributed to people's decreased level of engagement with the political process. By contrast, today's studies have examined the external communication environment as a source of cross-pressures. In this reexamination of the cross-pressures hypothesis, scholars have looked at communication sources such as interpersonal communication (Mutz, 2006), news content (Hmielowski, 2012), and political advertising (Keele & Wolak, 2008). This line of inquiry has focused on examining the extent to which use of supportive and opposing information is associated with outcome variables such as vote time decision (Matthes, 2012) and levels of political engagement (Dilliplane, 2011). In general, these studies show that hearing supportive information increases people's level of political engagement, whereas hearing opposing information tends to decrease engagement (Dilliplane, 2011).

The next step in developing a more comprehensive theoretical framework relative to the cross-pressures hypotheses is to examine intervening variables that could explain the relationship between hearing supportive (or opposing) information and levels of political engagement. For instance, a recent study by

Wojcieszak and her colleagues (2014) examined three potential mediators between news exposure and intention to engage in political behaviors. Specifically, they looked at whether cognitive, affective, and attitudinal variables could help explain the relationship between supportive and opposing content and political engagement. Their study found that supportive information increased engagement through these three mediating variables. To expand on the work by Wojcieszak et al. (2016) and her colleagues, this study looks at two additional intervening variables: ambivalence and strength of policy position.

The Cross-Pressure Hypothesis and Ambivalence

One variable that has garnered attention relative to the cross-pressures hypothesis is ambivalence. Ambivalence has been described as the idea that people can hold both positive and negative attitudes toward an object. The concept of ambivalence adds an additional layer of complexity to the existing conceptualization of attitudes by adding the dimension of coactivity (ambivalent or indifferent attitudes) to the existing dimension of "reciprocity" (positive or negative attitudes). The dimension of "coactivity" acknowledges that people can hold a weak attitude in which they have no positive or negative evaluations of an object (i.e., indifference) or they may hold a strong positive and strong negative attitude toward an object (i.e., ambivalent attitudes; Cacioppo, Gardner, & Berntson, 1997).

Media Use and Ambivalence. A number of studies have looked at the relationship between communication and attitudinal ambivalence. One consistent finding from these studies is that supportive information is associated with lower levels of ambivalence. Mutz (2006) found that hearing opinion-reinforcing information in one's social network strengthened existing attitudes and decreased ambivalence. Huckfeldt and his colleagues (2004) found similar results. Indeed, Republicans in a social network dominated by other Republicans reported more reasons for liking George W. Bush and disliking Al Gore. This imbalance of likes and dislikes translated into lower levels of ambivalence toward each candidate (Huckfeldt et al., 2004). This notion of supportive information decreasing ambivalence also has been applied to media use. Hutchens and her colleagues (2015) showed that use of supportive media was associated with lower levels of ambivalence.

By contrast, opinion-challenging information has been shown to increase ambivalence (Hutchens et al., 2015; Priester & Petty, 2001). Mutz (2006) and Huckfeldt et al. (2004) both found that hearing more oppositional information in one's social networks increases people's ambivalence (Huckfeldt et al., 2004). Media studies have shown similar results. Keele and Wolak (2008) showed that seeing ads from nonpreferred candidates increased levels of ambivalence toward presidential candidates. Hutchens and colleagues (2015) also found that use of opinion-challenging media outlets was associated with higher levels of ambivalence. In other words, research would suggest that there should be *a divergent interaction in that hearing information that supports people's views on climate change would be associated with lower levels of ambivalence, while hearing opposing information about the issue of climate change would be associated with higher levels of ambivalence* (H1).

Intervening Variables: Ambivalence and Policy Support. Scholars have added to the cross-pressures hypothesis by proposing that ambivalence could serve as a mediating variable between information use and measures of engagement (Hmielowski, 2012; Mutz, 2006). For example, Mutz (2006) showed evidence that ambivalence could serve as a mediating variable between information use and political engagement. Hmielowski (2012) provided a more direct test of this indirect effect. Specifically, he found that increased use of one-sided information reduced levels of ambivalence, which was associated with people picking a candidate earlier in the election cycle.

A common theme in these studies looking at ambivalence is the focus on general indicators of engagement (e.g., attend a political rally). Most of this research has yet to examine specific issues such as climate change. In this situation, an additional variable could help explain people's level of engagement. Specifically, people's strength of policy support could be an important component relative to understanding why hearing supportive and opposing information is associated with engagement. This component of strength of policy support is important when looking at ambivalence because holding conflicted attitudes has been shown to be a characteristic of a moderate electorate that is less engaged with the political process. Results have shown that ambivalence is associated with holding moderate political attitudes and holding less extreme evaluations of politicians and the policies they support (Lavine, Steenbergen, & Johnston, 2012). Therefore, we believe there should be *a negative relationship between ambivalence about climate change and strength of policy position for climate change mitigation policies, with higher levels of ambivalence associated with holding a weaker policy position* (H2).

Although research on ambivalence has yet to test whether strength of policy position mediates the indirect effects of ambivalence on engagement, findings suggest this could be the case. Ambivalence has been shown to both weaken people's policy position (Lavine et al., 2012) and decrease their levels of behavioral intentions relative to environmental issues (Castro et al., 2009). The missing link here is the relationship between strength of policy position and intention to take action. Researchers have proposed and shown that strength of policy position is an important factor relative to people's level of political engagement (Krosnick, 1988; Scheufele, Shanahan, & Kim, 2002). For instance,

Krosnick (1988) found that importantly held policy positions were associated with vote preference across a number of elections. Scheufele and his colleagues (2002) found that people who held a stronger policy position were more likely to be engaged in the political process. In general, we believe there should be *a positive relationship between strength of support for climate mitigation policies and intention to mobilize around the issue of climate change, with those holding a strong policy position being more likely to show intention to mobilize* (H3).

The Proposed Communication Process Model

This literature speaks to a larger communicative process in which ambivalence and strength of policy position, in part, explain the relationship between hearing supportive and opposing information and intention to take action in support of, or opposition to, climate change policies. In other words, consuming outlets that reinforce (or oppose) existing attitudes will increase (or decrease) ambivalence. These increases (or decreases) in ambivalence should result in individuals holding stronger or weaker global warming policy positions. Changes in strength of policy position, in turn, will likely increase (or decrease) people's intention to take action in support of, or opposition to, these policies. *In essence, we should see a conditional indirect relationship for supportive and opposing information on levels of engagement with the issue of climate change through ambivalence and strength of policy support* (H4).

METHOD

Data for this study were collected via the Internet from May 8 to May 12, 2011. Participants were recruited through Survey Sampling International's (SSI's) online survey panel. Panel participants are generally recruited via e-mail and receive monetary compensation for participating in studies. (See http://www.surveysampling.com/for more information on SSI panels.) A total of 1,735 respondents completed the survey. The survey consisted of a split ballot design, with half the respondents randomly assigned to receive questions about their attitudes toward climate change and the other half assigned to receive questions about plastic pollution. In all, 855 people completed the climate change survey. After removing anyone with missing data from the global warming sample, data from 828 survey respondents were included in the final analyses presented in this article. Although the SSI sample is not generalizable, it is heterogeneous and representative of the general population in terms of basic demographics such as age, education, race, and gender (see Online Appendix Table A1). Moreover, we are testing a theoretical process, which means we are more interested in making process inferences than population inferences. In other words, we are trying to build theory, which means we are more interested in replicating the results of the process proposed in the study. Indeed, as Hayes (2005) argued, "if the researcher does not want to make a specific statistical statement about a population, then the question of whether the sample is random or not becomes moot" (p. 41).

Independent Variables: Conservative and Nonconservative Media Use

In accordance with previous research looking at media use and beliefs about climate change, we separate our media use variables into conservative and nonconservative content (Feldman et al., 2012; Feldman et al., 2014; Hmielowski et al., 2014). We have decided to separate our media use into conservative and nonconservative outlets based on content analyses looking at how news outlets cover the issue of climate change. These studies have shown that less ideological (e.g., network news) and liberal outlets tend to emphasize that scientists agree that climate change is a manmade problem that deserves attention (Feldman et al., 2012; Nisbet, 2011). By contrast, conservative outlets tend to question the existence of climate change (Feldman et al., 2012; Nisbet, 2011). In our study, *conservative media use* was measured with three items that asked respondents how often they watch Fox News, listen to conservative radio, or visit conservative news websites ($\alpha = 0.76$, $M = 1.16$, $SD = 1.47$). *Nonconservative media use* was measured with six items that asked respondents how often they consume network news broadcasts (e.g., ABC, CBS, NBC), CNN, MSNBC, NPR, liberal radio programs, and liberal news websites ($\alpha = 0.75$, $M = 1.58$, $SD = 1.19$). Each item asked respondents how often they consumed each type of programming with the same 7-point scaling structure of 0 (*never*) to 6 (*daily*).

Mediating Variables

Ambivalence. Ambivalence toward climate change mitigation policies was assessed using split semantic differential items (Kaplan, 1972; Thompson, Zanna, & Griffin, 1995). These items separately assessed the costs and benefits of climate change mitigation policies relative to issues such as human health, technological innovation, the economy, and the environment, on a 7-point scale of 0 (*no benefits (or costs)*) to 6 (*a great deal of benefits (or costs)*). This conceptualization of ambivalence was taken from Poortinga and Pidgeon (2006), who used risks (e.g., costs) and benefits in their study focused on ambivalent attitudes toward genetically modified foods. The five cost items ($\alpha = 0.90$) and the five benefit ($\alpha = 0.92$) items were averaged together to make separate assessments of costs and benefits. The two averages were then put into Griffin's index to get a measure of ambivalence toward global climate change mitigation policies (Thompson et al., 1995) [Ambivalence = (Costs + Benefits)/

2—(|Costs—Benefits|)] (M = 2.38, SD = 2.05). For this scale, a higher score means higher levels of ambivalence.

Strength of Policy Position. Seven items were used to measure the strength of policy position. These items measured the extent to which an individual supported (or did not support) a series of proposed policies aimed at reducing the effects of global climate change on the environment. This set of items included policies supported by Democrats (e.g., implement a carbon tax) and Republicans (e.g., let the market decide). Because this study intends to measure strength of policy position, not the direction of support (i.e., support or do not support), the 7-point semantic differential scale of 1 (*strongly oppose*) to 7 (*strongly support*) was folded in half (Scheufele et al., 2002). Folding the item in half resulted in scores at either end of the scale (1 [*strongly oppose*] or 7 [*strongly support*]), to become holding a strong policy position (3), and scores at the midpoint of the scale (4), to become holding a weak policy position (0). All of the recoded items were averaged together to create an index of strength of policy position (α = 0.83, M = 1.63, SD = 0.78).

Dependent Variable

Intention to Take Action. Intention to take action was measured with five items asking people how likely they would be to engage in activities to support (or oppose) action on climate change. These items asked respondents how likely they would be to sign a position supporting (or opposing) legislation to limit greenhouse gases, contact their congressional representative about supporting (or opposing) legislation to limit greenhouse gases, write a letter to the editor to support (or oppose) action to limit greenhouse gases, attend a rally supporting (or opposing) legislation to limit greenhouse gases, and contribute money to an organization that supports (or opposes) action to limit greenhouse gases. All participants first were asked how much they support or oppose taking legislative action on climate change. It is important to note that this item was separate from the policy items outlined earlier in the article. Indeed, this was a filter item to provide respondents with appropriate questions about whether they would take supportive or oppositional action toward mitigation policies. Those who responded with *strongly support* or *somewhat support* were asked five questions about how likely they would be to engage in a range activities just described. Those who responded with *strongly oppose* or *somewhat oppose* were given the same questions, with the difference being that these items asked how likely they would be to engage in activities that oppose action on climate change. In the end, we had two indexes: one of intention to support policies and one of intention to oppose policies. Each set of items was averaged together to create an index of intention to take supportive or oppositional action. These two separate indexes were added together into one measure of intention to take political action (α for oppose = 0.91, α for support = 0.86, M = 3.65, SD = 1.46). Because our study is concerned only with people's intention to act, we believe it was appropriate to combine the opposing and supportive scales.

Moderating Variable

Ideology. *Political ideology* is the focal moderating variable for this article. As research has shown, conservatives and liberals generally hold opposing views on climate change. Indeed, conservatives tend to dismiss the idea that climate change is happening and is caused by humans, whereas liberals tend to believe the opposite (McCright & Dunlap, 2011). Based on this information, we believe that political ideology will serve as an appropriate moderator in this study. In essence, media that question the scientific consensus on climate change would serve as supportive information for conservatives and challenging information for liberals. By contrast, media that report on the scientific consensus would serve as supportive information for liberals and opinion-challenging information for conservatives. Ideology was measured with one item that asked respondents how they would describe their political views on a 7-point scale that ranged from 0 (*very liberal*) to 6 (*very conservative; M* = 3.11, *SD* = 1.53)

Control Variables

Media Use Control Variables. Two additional media use variables were included in the regression models as controls. *Newspaper use* averaged responses to questions asking how often respondents read national newspapers (e.g., the *New York Times*, the *Wall Street Journal*) and local newspapers (r = .23, M = 2.09, SD = 1.55). In addition, local TV news use was measured, with one item asking how frequently respondents watch a local news broadcast (M = 3.67, SD = 2.16). These three questions used the same 7-point scaling structure of 0 (*never read [or watch]*) to 6 (*watch [or read] daily*). We did not include these items as part of our measures of conservative and nonconservative media use for specific reasons. Newspaper use was excluded because the items did not specify the respondents' preferred newspaper. Because newspapers vary in terms of their ideological position, we decided to exclude this item from our two independent variables of interest. Similarly, we excluded local TV news use because coverage may vary a great deal across different regions of the country.

Environmental Control Variables. We also included four variables in our analyses that have been shown to be important for understanding attitudes and beliefs concerning environmental issues. *Religiosity* was measured with one item asking respondents how often they attend religious services during a week on a scale of 1 (*never*) to 6 (*more than once a week; M* = 2.58, *SD* = 1.74). *Opinion certainty* was measured with one item asking people the certainty of their position relative to global climate change on a scale of 1 (*very unsure*) to 7 (*very sure; M* = 4.70, *SD* = 1.08). *Environmental identity* was measured with one item that asked people whether they identify themselves as an environmentalist, using a 4-point scale of 0 (*do not identify as an environmentalist*) to 3 (*hold a strong environmental identity; M* = 1.26, *SD* = 0.89). *Risk perceptions* were measured by averaging together five items that asked respondents how much they thought global warming would harm plants and animals, people in other countries, people in the United States, people in your local community, and you and your family. These items used the same 0 (*no harm*) to 6 (*a great deal of harm*) scaling structure (α = 0.97, *M* = 3.64, *SD* = 1.75).

Demographic Control Variables. Demographic control variables were also included in our statistical analyses. *Age* was measured with one item asking people to report their age as of their last birthday (*M* = 49.29, *SD* = 16.23). *Education* was measured with one item on a 7- point scale of 1 (*eighth-grade education*) to 7 (*professional or doctoral degree* [e.g., PhD, MD, JD]; *M* = 4.97 [some college, no degree], *SD* = 1.38). *Income* was measured with one item that asked respondents to report their income before taxes, using a 9-point scale that ranged from 1 (*less than $10,000 a year*) to 9 (*more than $150,000 a year; M* = 4.86 [$40,000 to less than $50,000], *SD* = 2.15). Respondents also were asked to report their *race* (e.g., White, Black, Asian, etc.). This item was turned into a dichotomous variable for Whites and non-Whites (21.9% non-Whites). *Gender* was measured with a single item that asked people to indicate their biological sex (50.2% female).

Analysis Plan

These data were analyzed using simple regression and path analysis (Mplus Version 7). Simple regression was used to test the correlations between variables. Interactions were tested using the PROCESS model developed by Andrew Hayes (2013). Path analysis was used to test the conditional indirect effects proposed in this article. Use of path analysis in our serial mediation model allowed us to simultaneously test the conditional indirect effects of conservative and noncon-servative media use.[1] To get estimates of indirect effects and the confidence

---

[1] The full analysis included paths for media use and policy support. In addition, we accounted for the variance between our two media use items. To simplify the model in the article, we have not included these paths in **Figure 2**.

intervals associated with these indirect effects, we utilized bootstrapping. For each analysis, confidence intervals were generated via 5,000 bootstrapped estimates.

RESULTS

The first set of analyses looked at the relationship between our two media use variables and intention to take action on climate change policies. Results showed that greater use of conservative media was associated with greater intention to take action ($\beta = 0.199$, $SE = 0.041$, $p < .001$). However, results did not find a relationship between use of nonconservative media and intention to take action.

We next examined whether the relationship between our two media use items and ambivalence varies by political ideology. First, results show a statistically significant conservative media use by ideology interaction on ambivalence ($\beta = -0.175$, $SE = 0.028$, $p < .001$). A graph of the interaction shows that conservative news use was associated with lower levels of ambivalence among conservatives and moderates and increased levels of ambivalence among liberals. A probe of the interaction using the Johnson–Neyman technique found that this relationship was significant for conservatives (1 standard deviation above the mean on our measure of ideology) and moderates (mean). We did not find a significant relationship among liberals (an individual 1 standard deviation below the mean on ideology). However, the Johnson–Neyman technique revealed a significant relationship among those who identify themselves as *liberal* (1) or *very liberal* (0) on our ideology scale. These individuals showed higher levels of ambivalence as their use of conservative media increased (see Figure 1).

Our analysis also found a statistically significant nonconservative media use by ideology interaction on ambivalence ($\beta = 0.210$, $SE = 0.035$, $p < .001$). A graph of the interaction shows that nonconservative news use was associated with increased ambivalence among conservatives and moderates and decreased ambivalence among liberals (see Figure 1). A probe of the interaction found a statistically significant relationship among conservatives and moderates. We found only that use of nonconservative media decreased ambivalence among those identifying themselves as *liberal* (1) or *very liberal* (0) on our ideology scale. Overall, these findings show that use of supportive media is associated with lower levels of ambivalence, whereas opposing media is associated with higher levels of ambivalence (support for H1).

Results showed a negative relationship between ambivalence and strength of policy position, with higher levels of ambivalence associated with holding a less extreme position on global warming mitigation policies ($\beta = -0.062$, $SE = 0.013$, $p < .001$; support for H2). Results from the analysis also found that those with a

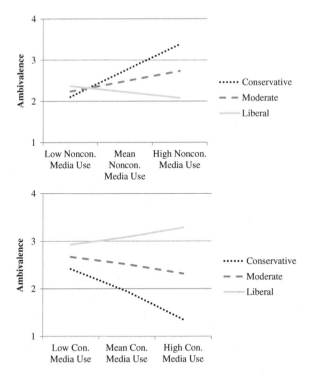

FIGURE 1 Media use by ideology on ambivalence graphs. Note: Low for conservative media is zero, low for non-conservative media is 1 *SD* below the mean.

stronger policy position showed greater intention to take action regarding climate change mitigation policies ($\beta = 0.480$, $SE = 0.067$, $p < .001$; support for H3).

Finally, analyses found support for our full communication model. Before talking about the full serial mediation model, we want to outline the specific indirect effects that make up the model. First, we found that ambivalence helped explain the relationship between media use and strength of policy position. Conservative media use had a positive indirect relationship among conservatives (point estimate = 0.023), 95% CI [0.014, 0.036], and moderates (point estimate = 0.009), 95% CI [0.002, 0.018]. We found the opposite effect among liberals, though only for those who identified themselves as "liberal" (point estimate = −0.014, [95% CI = −0.031–0.003]) and 'very liberal' (point estimate = −0.025), 95% CI [−0.047, −0.010], on our ideology scale. The opposite pattern was true for nonconservative media use. We found a negative indirect relationship for nonconservative media among conservatives (point estimate = −0.031), 95% CI [−0.050, −0.016], and moderates (point estimate = −0.013),

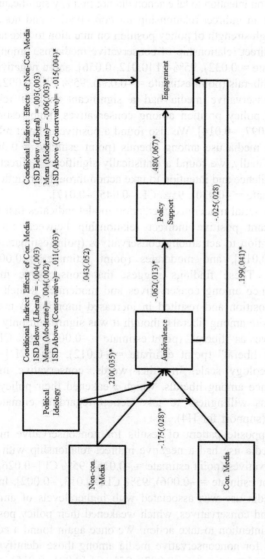

FIGURE 2 Proposed serial moderated mediated model.
Notes. Con. = conservative. * p < .05

95% CI [–0.026, –0.005], and a positive indirect relationship among those identifying themselves as "liberal" (point estimate = 0.014), 95% CI [0.003, 0.031], and "very liberal" (point estimate = 0.027), 95% CI [0.011, 0.051], on our ideology scale. Our examination of the conditional indirect relationships of our two media use variables through ambivalence on intention to take action did not find any significant findings.

Results did show an indirect relationship for conservative and nonconservative media use through strength of policy position on intention to take action. We found a positive indirect relationship of conservative media use among conservatives (point estimate = 0.032), 95% CI [0.012, 0.056], and a negative indirect relationship among liberals (point estimate = –0.054), 95% CI [–0.092, –0.022]. By contrast, nonconservative media had a significant indirect relationship through strength of policy position among conservatives (point estimate = –0.050), 95% CI [–0.097, –0.014]. We also found a positive indirect relationship for nonconservative media use among liberals (point estimate = 0.062), 95% CI [0.032, 0.100]. Finally, we found a statistically significant indirect relationship between ambivalence and intention to take action through strength of policy position (point estimate = –0.030), 95% CI [–0.045, –0.017].

A test of our full serial moderated mediation model indicates that there is a statistically significant positive indirect relationship between conservative media use and intention to act among conservatives (point estimate = 0.011), 95% CI [0.006, 0.018], and moderates (point estimate = 0.004), 95% CI [0.001, 0.009]. These findings suggest that conservative media use decreased ambivalence among conservatives and moderates, which strengthened their policy position and resulted in increased intention to take action. We found the opposite among liberals, though it was significant only for those identifying themselves as "liberal" (point estimate = –0.007), 95% CI [–0.015, –0.002], and "very liberal" (point estimate = –0.012), 95% CI [–0.024, –0.005], on our ideology scale. In other words, conservative media use increased ambivalence among liberals, which weakened their policy position and resulted in less willingness to take action regarding climate change mitigation policies (support for H4).

We found the opposite pattern of results for nonconservative media use. Nonconservative media use had a negative indirect relationship with intention to act among conservatives (point estimate = –0.015), 95% CI [–0.026, –0.008], and moderates (point estimate = –0.006), 95% CI [–0.013, –0.002]. In essence, nonconservative media use was associated with higher levels of ambivalence among moderates and conservatives, which weakened their policy position and resulted in lowered intention to take action. We once again found a conditional indirect relationship for nonconservative media among those identifying themselves as "liberal" (point estimate = 0.007), 95% CI [0.001, 0.015], and "very liberal" (point estimate = 0.013), 95% CI [0.005, 0.025]. These results show that nonconservative media use decreased ambivalence among liberals, which strengthened their policy position and resulted in increased intention to take political action (support for H4; for results of full model, see Online Appendix Table A2).

DISCUSSION

The results generally support our proposed model. We found a conditional relationship for both conservative and nonconservative media use through our two mediating variables. These results indicate that conservatives and moderates show lower levels of ambivalence as their use of conservative media increases. This decrease in levels of ambivalence in turn strengthens conservatives' policy position, which ultimately results in higher levels of intention to take action regarding climate change mitigation policies. By contrast, use of conservative media increases ambivalence among liberals, which weakens their strength of policy position and ultimately results in lower levels of intention to take action. We find the opposite pattern of results for nonconservative media use.

These findings make several contributions to the existing literature. First, this study helps extend the theoretical work being done on the cross-pressures hypothesis. It reexamines the work that has been done on ambivalence and adds strength of policy support as an additional mediating variable. Because this article is grounded in the theoretical work being done on the cross-pressures hypotheses, these results should replicate across contexts. However, scholars should test this model with other topics to determine how generalizable the results are beyond the issue of climate change.

Second, this study shows some potentially different relationships that can emerge by focusing on ambivalence. First, the inclusion of ambivalence could provide an explanation for why previous work has not shown indirect effects for opinion-challenging information through attitude strength (Wojcieszak et al., 2016). The use of attitude strength means that the "weak attitude" end of the scale could conflate indifference an ambivalence, which could make it more difficult to find a relationship between opposing information and holding a weak attitude. Second, the inclusion of ambivalence also may pick up findings that would be missed with more traditional measure of attitudes. A typical measure of attitudes that assesses the extent to which individuals hold negative or positive attitudes toward an object would miss the results showing that use of opinion-challenging information is associated with an increase in ambivalence. Instead, results simply would show movement toward the midpoint of a traditional attitude scale (Kaplan, 1972). This type of scale would likely show a correlation between liberals' use of conservative media and greater costs associated with climate change policies, which would likely show greater opposition to climate change policies and greater intention to take political action. Because the mid-point of traditional scales confounds ambivalence and indifference, it is important for scholars to determine how communication variables affect a wider range of attitudinal outcomes beyond the traditional scales that have dominated the social sciences. This is particularly important, given the results of this study that show focusing on ambivalence reveals a different set of results than would have been found with more traditional measures of attitudes.

The results of this study also provide important information regarding the ongoing debate as to whether ambivalence is a characteristic of an ideal- or confused citizenry. Some scholars point to results—showing that ambivalence leads people to engage in systematic processing of information (Bromer, 1998) and to rely less on heuristics such as party identification when making decisions (Basinger & Lavine, 2005)—as evidence that ambivalence is a characteristic of an ideal citizenry. However, findings—showing that ambivalence causes people to delay decisions (Hmielowski, 2012), leads to inconsistences between their attitudes and the policies and politicians that they support (Fournier, 2005), and weakens the relationship between attitudes and behaviors (Castro et al., 2009)—suggest ambivalence may be an indicator of a confused citizenry. The results of this study show higher ambivalence is associated with holding a weaker policy position, and reduced intention to act suggests that holding opposing attitudes is more characteristic of a confused citizenry. Future research should continue to examine this issue.

Although this study provides support for our communication process model, some questions remain. One interesting finding is that conservatives and moderates tend to show greater shifts in ambivalence compared to their liberal counterparts. The changes in moderates' opinions and behavior make sense, in that they tend to be less ideological and hold moderate attitudes (Ellis & Stimson, 2012). The results for conservatives, though interesting and potentially counter-intuitive, are not new. Feldman and colleagues (2012) found a similar result in their study looking at the relationship between news use and climate change attitudes. A potential explanation for the difference between liberals and conservatives comes from recent research looking at the foundations of ideology among the U.S. electorate. Ellis and Stimson (2012) showed that liberals are more consistent in their commitment to core ideological tenets compared to conservatives. They also argue that people who identify themselves as conservatives comprise two groups (Ellis & Stimson, 2012): libertarians who believe in the importance of small government, and religious fundamentalists who hold culturally conservative views toward issues such as abortion and gay marriage. Given the disparate nature of those identifying themselves as conservative, it is possible that this group has greater potential to shift attitudes compared to their liberal counterparts. Indeed, it could be that these groups place importance on different aspects of this issue, which makes them more malleable depending on the content of the message. In essence, libertarians might be more persuaded by messages that emphasize the potential increase in government intervention that could occur as climate change problems begin to manifest themselves across the country. By contrast, religious individuals might be more persuaded by messages emphasizing the need for humans to take care of God's creation (i.e., Earth).

Although the generalizability of these results is limited, they speak to two important practical findings. First, our findings reveal a challenge for those focused on climate change communication. It would seem that climate contrarians have an easier task than those concerned about addressing climate change. In essence, the current propaganda of instilling fear, uncertainty, and doubt about the issue of climate change seems to be an effective strategy. Studies have shown that confusion often reduces people's beliefs that it is possible to solve the issue of climate change (Aitken, Chapman, & McClure, 2011). Our study shows that conflicting attitudes, which could be a type of uncertainty, may have a similar effect. In essence, contrarians only need to create doubt by increasing the salience of conflicting attitudes in memory. By contrast, organizations concerned about climate change are obligated to reduce ambivalence and create strong, consistent attitudes among the public in order to mobilize them to take action. Although some people voice their concern that hearing supportive information leads to problematic outcomes such as polarization (Levendusky, 2013), these findings suggest that supportive information may be important in increasing engagement.

These results also speak to the potential opportunity to change people's opinions about this urgent environmental issue. Scholars have shown that ambivalence increases the potential for persuasion (Zemborain & Johar, 2007). In combination with studies showing that holding conflicting attitudes leads people to rely less on heuristic cues when processing information, people high in ambivalence could pay closer attention to the information about climate change. Results showing that conservatives hold more conflicting attitudes and a weaker policy position based on their use of nonconservative media speak to this potential benefit. However, our results also show that conservative news outlets increase ambivalence among liberals, which may result in these individuals seeking information from climate skeptics and in turn thwart large-scale action on climate change.

As with any research, limitations of the study need to be addressed. The most prominent weakness is the use of cross-sectional data. Cross-sectional data prevent us from examining the causal direction of these relationships. However, experimental work and two-wave survey data have shown that media messages are associated with changes in people's attitudes about global warming (Feldman et al., 2014; Hmielowski et al., 2014). Future researchers should continue to collect longitudinal data to examine these relationships over time. A second limitation of this study is the use of items asking about behavioral intentions instead of actual behaviors. Research generally has shown that behavioral intentions do not always mean that people will engage in these actual behaviors (Ajzen, 2011). Therefore, future researchers should measure actual behaviors through self-report questions or actual behaviors in a lab setting.

In conclusion, our study finds support for our communication process model examining the conditional indirect effects of divergent media outlets on engagement through ambivalence and strength of policy support. Indeed, it seems that increasing engagement could be a difficult task. Because people need strong, consistent attitudes to get involved with supporting or opposing policies, discourse from those who oppose action may raise doubt to hinder engagement, as these oppositional pieces of information increase people's ambivalence. Although some have emphasized the importance of hearing the other side and holding conflicting attitudes toward a topic, this study speaks to a potential problem associated with hearing opposing information. Specifically, conflicting attitudes may depress levels of engagement.

SUPPLEMENTAL DATA

Supplemental data for this article can be accessed here.

REFERENCES

Aitken, C., Chapman, R., & McClure, J. (2011). Climate change, powerlessness, and the commons dilemma: Assessing New Zealanders' preparedness to act. *Global Environmental Change, 21*, 752–760.

Ajzen, I. (2011). Theory of planned behavior. In P. A. M. Van Lange, A. W. Kruglanski, & E. T. Higgins (Eds.), *Handbook of the theories of social psychology: Volume One* (pp. 438–459). Thousand Oaks, CA: Sage.

Basinger, S. J., & Lavine, H. (2005). Ambivalence, information, and electoral choice. *American Political Science Review, 99*(2), 169–184.

Bromer, P. (1998). Ambivalent attitudes and information processing. *Swiss Journal of Psychology, 57*(4), 225–234.

Cacioppo, J. T., Gardner, W. L., & Berntson, G. G. (1997). Beyond bipolar conceptualizations and measures: The case of attitudes and evaluative space. *Personality and Social Psychological Review, 1*(1), 3–25.

Castro, P., Garrido, M., Reis, E., & Menezes, J. (2009). Ambivalence and conservation behaviour: An exploratory study on the recycling of metal cans. *Journal of Environmental Psychology, 29*(1), 24–33. doi:10.1016/j.jenvp.2008.11.003

Dilliplane, S. (2011). All the news you want to hear: The impact of partisan news exposure on political participation. *Public Opinion Quarterly, 75*(2), 287–316. doi:10.1093/poq/nfr006

Ellis, C., & Stimson, J. A. (2012). *Ideology in America*. New York, NY: Cambridge University Press.

Feldman, L., Maibach, E. W., Roser-Renouf, C., & Leiserowitz, A. (2012). Climate on cable: The nature and impact of global warming coverage on Fox News, CNN, and MSNBC. *The International Journal of Press/Politics, 17*(1), 3–31. doi:10.1177/1940161211425410

Feldman, L., Myers, T., Hmielowski, J. D., & Leiserowitz, A. (2014). The mutual reinforcement of media selectivity and effects: Testing the reinforcing spirals framework in the context of global warming. *Journal of Communication, 64*(4), 590–611. doi:10.1111/jcom.12108

Fournier, P. (2005). Ambivalence and attitude change in vote choice: Do campaign switchers experience internal conflict? In C. C. Craig, & M. D. Martinez (Eds.), *Ambivalence, politics, and public policy* (pp. 83–102). New York, NY: Palgrave Macmillan.

Hayes, A. F. (2005). *Statistical methods for communication science.* Mahwah, NJ: Erlbaum.

Hayes, A. F. (2013). *Introduction to mediation, moderation, and conditional process analysis.* New York, NY: Guilford Press.

Hmielowski, J. D. (2012). Intramedia moderation, electoral ambivalence, and electoral decision making. *Mass Communication & Society, 15*(3), 454–477. doi:10.1080/15205436.2011.616640

Hmielowski, J. D., Feldman, L., Myers, T., Leiserowitz, A., & Maibach, E. (2014). An attack on science? Media use, trust in scientists, and perceptions of global warming. *Public Understanding of Science, 23*(7), 866–883. doi:10.1177/0963662513480091

Holbert, R. L., Kwak, N., & Shah, D. V. (2003). Environmental concern, patterns of television viewing, and pro-environmental behaviors: Integrating models of media consumption and effects. *Journal of Broadcasting & Electronic Media, 47*(2), 177–196.

Huckfeldt, R., Mendez, J. M., & Osborn, T. (2004). Disagreement, ambivalence, and engagement: The political consequences of heterogeneous networks. *Political Psychology, 25*(1), 65–95.

Hutchens, M. J., Hmielowski, J. D., & Beam, M. A. (2015). Rush, Rachel, and Rx: Modeling partisan media's influence on structural knowledge of healthcare policy. *Mass Communication and Society, 18*(2), 123–143.

IPCC (2013). *Intergovernmental panel on climate change, fifth assessment report.* Retrieved from http://www.ipcc.ch

Jamieson, K. H., & Hardy, B. W. (2014). Leveraging scientific credibility about Arctic sea ice trends in a polarized political environment. *Proceedings of the National Academy of Sciences, 111* (Supplement 4), 13598–13605.

Kaplan, K. J. (1972). On the ambivalence-indifference in attitude theory and measurement: A suggested modification of the semantic differential technique. *Psychological Bulletin, 77*, 361–372.

Keele, L., & Wolak, J. (2008). Contextual sources of ambivalence. *Political Psychology, 29*(5), 653–673. doi:10.1111/j.1467-9221.2008.00659.x

Krosnick, J. A. (1988). The role of attitude importance in social evaluation: A study of policy preferences, presidential candidate evaluations, and voting behavior. *Journal of Personality and Social Psychology, 55*(2), 196–210.

Lavine, H., Steenbergen, M., & Johnston, C. (2012). *The ambivalent partisan: How critical loyalty promotes democracy.* New York, NY: Oxford University Press.

Lazarsfeld, P. F., Berelson, B., & Gaudet, H. (1968). *The people's choice: How the voter makes up his mind in a presidential campaign.* New York, NY: Columbia University Press.

Leiserowitz, A., Maibach, E., Roser-Renouf, C., & Hmielowski, J. D. (2012). *Americans' actions to conserve energy, reduce waste, and limit global warming: March 2012.* New Haven, CT: Yale University and George Mason University, Yale Project on Climate Change Communication. Retrieved from http://environment.yale.edu/files/BehaviorMarch2012.pdf

Levendusky, M. (2013). *How partisan media polarize America.* Chicago, IL: University of Chicago Press.

Lupia, A. (2013). Communicating science in politicized environments. *Proceedings of the National Academy of Sciences, 110*(Suppl. 3), 14048–14054.

Maio, G. R., Bell, D. W., & Esses, V. M. (1996). Ambivalence and persuasion: The processing of messages about immigrant groups. *Journal of Experimental Social Psychology, 32*, 513–536.

Matthes, J. (2012). Exposure to counterattitudinal news coverage and the timing of voting decisions. *Communication Research, 39*(2), 147–169. doi:10.1177/0093650211402322

McCright, A. M., & Dunlap, R. E. (2011). The politicization of climate change and polarization in the American public's view of global warming, 2001–2010. *The Sociological Quarterly, 52*, 155–194. doi:10.1111/j.1533-8525.2011.01198.x

Moser, S. C. (2010). Communicating climate change: History, challenges, process and future directions. *Wiley Interdisciplinary Reviews: Climate Change, 1*(1), 31–53. doi:10.1002/wcc.11

Mutz, D. C. (2006). *Hearing the other side: Deliberative versus participatory democracy.* New York, NY: Cambridge University Press.

Nisbet, E. C., Cooper, K. E., & Garrett, R. K. (2015). The partisan brain: How dissonant science messages lead conservatives and liberals to (Dis) trust science. *The ANNALS of the American Academy of Political and Social Science, 658*(1), 36–66. doi:10.1177/0002716214555474

Nisbet, M. C. (2011). *Climate shift: Clear vision for the next decade of public debate.* Retrieved from http://climateshiftproject.org/report/climate-shift-clear-vision-for-the-next-decade-of-public-debate/#climate-shift-clear-vision-for-the-next-decade-of-public-debate

Poortinga, W., & Pidgeon, N. F. (2006). Exploring the structure of attitudes toward genetically modified food. *Risk Analysis, 26*(6), 1707–1719. doi:10.1111/j.1539-6924.2006.00828.x

Priester, J. R., & Petty, R. E. (2001). Extending the bases of subjective attitudinal ambivalence: Interpersonal and intrapersonal antecedents of evaluative tension. *Journal of Personality and Social Psychology, 80*(1), 19–34.

Scheufele, D. A., Shanahan, J., & Kim, S. E. (2002). Think about it this way: Attribute agenda-setting function of the press and the public's evaluation of a local issue. *Journalism & Mass Communication Quarterly, 79*(1), 7–25.

Thompson, M. M., Zanna, M. P., & Griffin, D. W. (1995). Let's not be indifferent about (attitudinal) ambivalence. In R. E. Petty & J. A. Krosnick (Eds.), *Attitude strength: Antecedents and consequences* (pp. 361–386). Mahwah, NJ: Erlbaum.

Wojcieszak, M., Bimber, B., Feldman, L., & Stroud, N. J. (2016). Partisan News and Political Participation: Exploring Mediated Relationships. *Political Communication, 33*(2), 241–260.

Zemborain, M. R., & Johar, G. V. (2007). Attitudinal ambivalence and openness to persuasion: A framework for interpersonal influence. *Journal of Consumer Research, 33*(4), 506–514. doi:10.1086/510224

Communicating Sustainability Online: An Examination of Corporate, Nonprofit, and University Websites

Holly Ott

School of Journalism & Mass Communications
University of South Carolina

Ruoxu Wang and Denise Bortree

College of Communications
The Pennsylvania State University

Sustainability, here defined as environmental quality and well-being, has emerged as a core business strategy and a focal area of investigation among communication scholars. This study analyzed sustainability landing pages on websites of top corporations, non-profits, and colleges/universities for the types of sustainability content presented. Comparisons are made between organization types. Few nonprofits in the sample provided sustainability content; however, nearly all universities and more than half of the corporations had a designated sustainability landing page on their websites. Findings suggest that organizations are promoting certain content, but fewer than 40% quantify their sustainability claims on any topic. Implications about the role of these communication forms for sustainability programs are discussed.

Companies and organizations that recognize the benefits of "going green" are embracing the opportunity to incorporate sustainability into core business functions and initiatives and report on these initiatives to key stakeholders. From recycling programs to developing college and university "Green Teams," companies and organizations are seeking ways to build efforts related to the goals of social and ecological sustainability (Frankental, 2001).

Scholars have noted that sustainability has become "commonplace in organizations" (Craig & Allen, 2013, p. 292) and recognized as a "dominant issue across the globe" (Ki & Shin, 2014, p. 2). Furthermore, as Bortree (2014) suggested, a popular trend in corporate communication now includes sustainability as a key business strategy, which has implications for sustainability communication programs in practice. Companies are enhancing sustainability initiatives and goals in their operations and practices. Corporations are adopting sustainability as a core business strategy to help maintain and regenerate critical resources. According to KPMG (2011), 55% of companies have established a sustainability strategy, and another 12% are in the process of creating one. Higher education institutions also are making efforts through the development of recycling and energy awareness campaigns, supporting student sustainability projects, and more actively involving key stakeholders in sustainability efforts.

Among the many benefits of enhancing sustainability strategy are increased satisfaction among multiple stakeholders (Klettner, Clarke, & Boersma, 2014; Mincer, 2008), higher purchase intention among consumers (Juwaheer, Pudaruth, & Noyaux, 2012; Sass, 2008), greater legitimacy and admiration of the organization (Bortree, 2009; Thomas & Lamm, 2012), enhanced company reputation (Kim & Lee, 2012), stronger relationships with publics (Hall, 2006), and greater levels of trust and positive word-of-mouth communication (Hong & Rim, 2010).

However, to a large extent, what and how companies, organizations, and higher education institutions are communicating about sustainability initiatives remains unknown. That is, what information is available to the public? Scholars have argued that the Internet has become a key medium through which companies communicate information and that stakeholders are most frequently turning to websites to learn about environmental issues (Bortree, 2011). Furthermore, Capriotti and Moreno (2007) argued that an organization's website is a key channel for communicating information to stakeholders. Scholars have examined how companies have communicated corporate social responsibility (CSR) efforts through their websites (Capriotti & Moreno, 2007; Kim & Ferguson, 2014; Kim & Rader, 2010; Signitzer & Prexl, 2008), but a thorough investigation of how sustainability is communicated through websites across multiple sectors has not been conducted.

The purpose of this study is to fill the gap in sustainability communication research by examining sustainability content on websites among corporations, nonprofits, and colleges/universities to determine (a) what sustainable topics are (or are not) communicated to key stakeholders; (b) how and to what extent sustainable content is communicated; and (c) how sustainability communication efforts differ among corporations, nonprofits, and colleges/universities.

BUILDING DIALOGUE ABOUT SUSTAINABILITY COMMUNICATION

Defining Sustainability

Sustainability commonly is defined as "development that meets the needs of the present without compromising the ability of future generations to meet their own needs" (World Commission on Environment and Development, 1987, p. 41) or more recently as "economic development that creates value for customers, shareholders, stakeholders, and society by designing and operating business in a way that aligns with ecosystems, in service of human prosperity, today and in the future" (Figge, 2011, para. 4). Organizations that formally report their sustainability goals and achievements focus primarily on their impacts on the environment, though consideration also is given to social impacts (Global Reporting Initiative [GRI], n.d.).

Historically, several terms have been used to refer to aspects of sustainability communication (Ki & Shin, 2014). These include CSR communication, green communication, environmental sustainability, global responsibility communication, social responsibility communication, and corporate sustainability communication (Signitzer & Prexl, 2008). Although the lines between sustainability and CSR may appear to be blurry, an article published by Montiel (2008) acts as a reference point for distinguishing the two concepts. Through an analysis of the leading business literature, Montiel found that historically, sustainability has been defined in two ways: as environmental sustainability and as triple bottom line—social, environmental, and financial. Both types of sustainability are deeply rooted in ecological strategies of an organization, but environmental sustainability focuses only on the ways the organization conducts business in relationship to the environment. Sustainability typically is concerned with management of resources to improve profitability by reducing waste. It focuses on making decisions today that do not negatively impact the organization's ability to operate in the future (Van Marrewijk, 2003). Modern definitions position sustainability as a key business strategy, as suggested by Bortree (2014), but also suggest environmental sustainability can be a dimension of CSR, depending on how sustainability is defined by the organization.

Other terms have been used interchangeably with sustainability communication. Most recently, Ki and Shin (2014) proposed a new term, *organization sustainability communication* (OSC), emphasizing that the term "organization" is "more inclusive and suitable" (p. 4) and not limited to only communication efforts in the corporate sector. Although this study broadly uses the term "sustainability communication," it is suitable to apply Ki and Shin's OSC term to this study, as the purpose of the study is to examine environmental sustainability content on websites across three sectors:

corporate, nonprofit, and higher education institutions. Furthermore, because scholars have referred to sustainability communication, or OSC, using several terms, this study seeks to determine how companies, organizations, and institutions are most commonly defining environmental sustainability on websites and what they are communicating to publics about their environmental sustainability initiatives specifically on sustainability landing pages. The current study limits its definition of sustainability to include environmental actions and communication (environmental sustainability) only, not including social and non-ecological philanthropic efforts of organizations.

Sustainability Message Content

With regard to the amount and type of sustainability content that companies, organizations, and institutions provide on websites, it is important to consider message factors and various communication approaches to disseminating content. With regard to message content, persuasion scholars have found evidence to support the argument that statistical evidence generally is more impactful to audiences over time (Baesler & Burgoon, 1994). For this study, it is important to consider how different types of content may impact perceptions of key stakeholders, as messages are capable of shaping stakeholder perceptions of company reputation (Du, Bhattacharya, & Sen, 2010) and how empirical evidence might enhance communication strategy.

Prior research has investigated efforts to measure sustainability in companies and organizations, as well as approaches for advancing sustainability in higher education through research (Fien, 2002). However, conclusions from existing studies have suggested that much of the information available lacks empirical evidence (Shriberg, 2002). Although it is likely that similar trends exist in corporate and nonprofit settings, existing research does not provide substantive information that indicates what type of content exists on sustainability websites. Therefore, there is a need for research that further explores what corporations, nonprofits, and colleges/universities are communicating on websites. Specifically, this investigation adds to existing research that has examined CSR communication efforts on websites (Capriotti & Moreno, 2007; Kim & Ferguson, 2014; Kim & Rader, 2010; Signitzer & Prexl, 2008) by examining a new, related area—how sustainability is communicated through this particular communication channel. As scholars have found that effective communication about CSR activities and efforts can impact public perception about a company or organization, the same arguments can apply in the area of sustainability communication. To investigate this information, the first two research questions are posed:

RQ1: How are companies communicating about their environmental sustainability efforts through content on websites?
RQ2: Which sustainability topics are communicated the most (generally and empirically) through company, organization, and institutional websites?

Sustainability Communication Reporting

Although companies, nonprofits, and colleges/universities are not required to adhere to specific reporting standards, many use the Sustainability Tracking, Assessment and Rating System (STARS) reporting framework and the GRI standards for sustainability communication and reporting (de Lange, 2013; Manetti & Toccafondi, 2014; Val, Zinenko, & Montiel, 2011). GRI is a leading organization in the sustainability field, and according to its website, GRI (n.d.) "promotes the use of sustainability reporting as a way for organizations to become more sustainable and contribute to sustainable development" (para. 2). According to the STARS website, this self-reporting framework provides guidelines for colleges and universities to measure their sustainability performance (Association for the Advancement of Sustainability in Higher Education, n.d.). This study refers to the GRI and STARS categories as the "gold standard" for sustainability communication and thus uses several categories included in these frameworks to drive the study methodology. Therefore, although a lack of required standardized reporting makes it difficult to compare detailed reporting methods across multiple sectors, this study's inclusion of GRI and STARS categories as measures allows for an analysis of how companies, organizations, and colleges/universities are communicating about sustainability in accordance with "gold standard" reporting methods. With consideration to sustainability communication practices, message content, and reporting guidelines, the following research question is posed:

> RQ3: Which sector (nonprofit organizations, colleges/universities, or corporations) is communicating about sustainability content on websites in accordance with GRI/STARS guidelines?

Communicating Sustainability to Stakeholders

Drawing on Freeman's (1984) stakeholder theory, it is important to consider key audiences when communicating about sustainability initiatives. An important component of stakeholder theory is that, by definition, the environment is considered a stakeholder. The inclusion of the environment in this definition has impacted how organizations structure CSR and sustainability programs and activities. With regard to sustainability communication, it is important to consider what information is provided to key stakeholders, as stakeholder influence may impact the outcomes of sustainability efforts. According to Craig and Allen (2013), "employees must be aware of their organization's sustainability initiatives, and the impact of such initiatives" (pp. 296–297). Arguably, this same philosophy applies to external stakeholders with regard to the attitudes, behavioral intentions, and impact they may have on a given sustainability initiative's success. Craig and Allen also suggest that increased stakeholder involvement in sustainability initiatives may lead to an increased level of interest and support of sustainability initiatives among these audiences. Therefore, it is logical to suggest that companies, organizations, and colleges/universities should engage in sustainability activities that involve key publics. With this suggestion in mind, the final research question is posed:

> RQ4: What types of organizations (colleges/universities, nonprofits, or corporations) are communicating the most information about sustainability initiatives that include employees and stakeholder involvement?

METHOD

Research Design

To answer the research questions, this study examined sustainability landing pages on websites of top-ranked colleges/universities, corporations, and nonprofit organizations. Content analysis was used to analyze sustainability content and how organizations are defining and communicating sustainability on websites. As this study is exploratory in nature, limiting the examination to sustainability landing pages was only a coding decision based on previous literature that solely focused on landing pages in web usability, sustainability, and other related studies (Marchiori, Inversini, & Cantoni, 2010; Zoch, Collins, & Sisco, 2008).

Sampling Procedure

This study examined 300 websites. A random sample of 100 college/university sites was selected from the top 200 ranked colleges/universities listed on the U.S. News Top National Universities (Public and Private) 2014 Best Colleges rankings list. The 2014 list is based on 2013 data. Next, a random sample of 100 nonprofit organizations' websites was selected from the top 200 nonprofits included in The Philanthropy 200 (from *The Chronicle of Philanthropy*) in 2013. Nonprofit organizations with an ".edu" website address were not included in this category so as to avoid overlapping with the college/university category. Finally, a random sample of 100 company websites was selected from the 2013 *Fortune 200*.

Coding Scheme

The analysis was split into two major categories: sustainability content reporting and sustainability communication features. In addition, structural information about each website was analyzed, such as the location of the sustainability page relative to the home page and the sustainability landing page title.

Structural Information. First, the presence or absence of a sustainability landing page on a company's, organization's, or institution's website was coded.

A sustainability landing page was defined as one that is clearly titled "sustainability" or one that refers to "sustainability" in the site title. Related pages with titles such as "corporate responsibility" or "social responsibility" were not included in this definition, as the goal was to identify a sustainability landing page. The authors reasoned that someone who is looking for sustainability information would likely come to a page with that word in the title and not search throughout a website for content under other topics. In addition, because the study examined content from STARS and GRI sustainability reporting systems, the authors believed that content would be collected into a sustainability section of the website. Coders were instructed to search an entire company's, organization's, or institution's main website to search for a sustainability landing page. If a sustainability landing page was identified, the URL was noted and the exact page title was recorded (e.g., "Sustainability" or "Sustainable Initiatives"). Finally, coders identified the site location of the sustainability page. That is, coders identified under which section (from the main website/home page) the sustainability landing page was listed: top of home page, bottom of home page, About Us, corporate social responsibility, not visible (i.e., had to use the Search function to find the sustainability page), or other.

Sustainability Content Reporting. Sustainability content categories were constructed based on categories that are included in the GRI reporting categories and the STARS reporting framework. Based on the sustainability areas emphasized by the GRI and STARS, the following sustainability categories were constructed for this study: research; campus or company engagement; public engagement; air and climate; buildings; dining services/food; energy; grounds; purchasing; transportation; waste; water; diversity and affordability, health, well-being, and work; curriculum; and investment.

Each category was coded based on the type of information included on the sustainability website. Therefore, for each sustainability category, coders indicated whether there was no information about a particular category (e.g., air and climate) on the sustainability website (No information = 0), general information only (General information = 1), or empirical data/hard numbers (Empirical data = 2). General information about a category was defined as information that includes the category name/term (e.g., waste) and information about the company's, organization's, or institution's involvement with that topic. The following example was provided to coders for reference: "We are committed to reducing waste and improving energy efficiency." Information that included empirical data (hard numbers) was defined as information that is specific, quantifiable, and measurable. An example was provided to coders for reference: "We are committed to reducing waste and improving energy by 10 percent by 2016."

Sustainability Communication Features. As an extension of the sustainability content categories just described, the presence or absence of

13 additional dimensions was coded in an attempt to identify what sustainability communication features were included on a company's, organization's, or institution's sustainability website. The 13 items that were coded (1 = yes; 0 = no) included a definition for sustainability, information regarding a sustainability strategic plan, a downloadable sustainability report, information about sustainability programming, information about sustainability educational opportunities, information about sustainability research, employee involvement in sustainability initiatives, customer/stakeholder involvement in sustainability initiatives, links to news articles or press releases about sustainability, videos about sustainability, features that support interactive dialogue (e.g., interactive surveys, webchats, social networks, etc.), a company/organizational/institutional blog, and a glossary of sustainability terms and expressions. The codebook was refined and revised by several rounds of discussions and testing using a small portion of the sample.

Intercoder Reliability Test and Coding

Two coders, one of this study's co-authors and one other graduate student, were trained through coding practices and discussion after the codebook was completed. A mutual understanding of the codebook was achieved before the intercoder reliability test. To test intercoder reliability, two coders independently coded 20% of the websites that were randomly selected from the sample. Therefore, 60 websites (20 college/university websites, 20 corporation websites, and 20 nonprofit organization websites) were randomly selected using a stratified random sampling method to test intercoder reliability. Coder reliability was calculated by using Krippendorff's alpha (Hayes & Krippendorff, 2007). Krippendorff's alpha for all coding categories ranged from .80 to 1. Thus, the overall reliability was satisfactory. The level of reliability for each coding category reached above the acceptable threshold—.80, as suggested by Riffe, Lacy, and Fico (2013). After the intercoder reliability test, the coders independently coded the remaining websites.

RESULTS

Descriptive Results

Among the 300 coded websites, more than half of the websites (53%, $N = 159$) had sustainability landing pages. This included 93 university websites, 62 company websites, and four nonprofit websites. Among the websites with sustainability landing pages, about 40.3% had sustainability landing pages on the main website itself. There was little consistency in where the links to the sustainability landing page were located. About 18.2% of the websites placed the sustainability link under the About Us section. About 14.5% of the websites' sustainability landing pages were CSR related. About 8.2% of the websites placed the link to the sustainability landing page at the top of home page. About 8.2% of the websites placed it at the bottom of the home page. About 10.7% of the websites placed it in other locations (i.e. middle of home page, A to Z index).

Major Findings

RQ1 asked how companies and organizations are communicating about environmental sustainability through website content. To answer RQ1, a series of frequency analyses were employed. As shown in Table 1, only 12% of the 300 websites included a definition of sustainability. About 40.7% included information about sustainability strategic plan/goals. In addition, 33.3% included downloadable sustainability reports, 34.3% had information about programming, 32.3% had information about sustainability education, 27% had sustainability research information, 31% addressed employee involvement in sustainability initiatives, and 31.7% included customer/ stakeholder involvement in sustainability initiatives. As well, 33.7% of the websites contained links to news articles/press releases, 18.3% had videos about sustainability, and 27% included interactive features. Blog features were included on 8.7% of the websites. However, only one of the 300 websites (0.3%) had a glossary explaining sustainability (see Table 1).

RQ2 was raised to determine which sustainable topics were communicated the most through nonprofit, corporation, and college/university websites. To answer RQ2, a series of frequency analyses were performed. As shown in Table 2a, the

TABLE 1
Presence of Sustainability Communication Features on Websites

Sustainability Communication Features	Total[a]	Nonprofit[b]	Company[c]	University[d]
Sustainability strategic plan/goals	40.7%	3.0%	47.0%	72.0%
Programming	34.3%	4.0%	14.0%	85.0%
Links to news articles/press release	33.7%	2.0%	37.0%	62.0%
Downloadable sustainability report	33.3%	0.0%	40.0%	60.0%
Sustainability education	32.3%	3.0%	15.0%	79.0%
Customer/stakeholder involvement	31.7%	0.0%	32.0%	63.0%
Employee involvement	31.0%	1.0%	37.0%	55.0%
Sustainability research	27.0%	2.0%	10.0%	69.0%
Interactive features	27.0%	1.0%	32.0%	48.0%
Video about sustainability	18.3%	1.0%	20.0%	34.0%
Definition of sustainability	12.0%	1.0%	4.0%	31.0%
Blog	8.7%	2.0%	8.0%	16.0%
Glossary explain sustainability terms	0.3%	0.0%	1.0%	0.0%

[a]$N = 300$. [b]$n = 100$. [c]$n = 100$. [d]$n = 100$.

TABLE 2A
Presence of Sustainability Content (Number of Topics)

Sustainability Topics	Overall[a]	Nonprofit[b]	Company[c]	University[d]
Waste	50.0%	4.0%	65.0%	81.0%
Energy	48.0%	3.0%	64.0%	77.0%
Building	45.3%	4.0%	56.0%	76.0%
Water	45.3%	5.0%	60.0%	71.0%
Air and climate	39.0%	3.0%	59.0%	55.0%
Transportation	39.0%	1.0%	45.0%	71.0%
Sustainability curriculum	38.3%	5.0%	30.0%	80.0%
Campus engagement with sustainability	35.6%	0.0%	24.0%	83.0%
Public engagement with sustainability	35.0%	2.0%	57.0%	46.0%
Grounds	34.0%	2.0%	47.0%	53.0%
Sustainability research	31.6%	4.0%	19.0%	72.0%
Purchasing	31.3%	2.0%	52.0%	40.0%
Dining services/food	31.0%	1.0%	21.0%	71.0%
Investment	27.3%	3.0%	54.0%	25.0%
Health, well-being, and work	17.0%	4.0%	34.0%	13.0%
Diversity and affordability	10.3%	1.0%	24.0%	6.0%

[a]$N = 300$. [b]$n = 100$. [c]$n = 100$. [d]$n = 100$.

range of all 16 sustainable topics presented by the three types of websites (nonprofit, corporation, and college/university) was 10.3% to 50%. Specifically, the most communicated topic was waste (50%). For nonprofit websites, the range of all 16 sustainable topics presented on the site was 0% to 5%. The most communicated topics were water (5%) and sustainability curriculum (5%). For corporation websites, the range of all 16 sustainable topics presented on the site was 19% to 65%. The most communicated topics were waste (65%) and energy (64%). For college/ university websites, the range of all 16 sustainable topics presented on the site was 6% to 83%. The most communicated topics were campus engagement with sustainability (83%) and waste (80%).

To fully answer this research question, a frequency analysis was run to determine how often college/universities, nonprofits, and corporations provided empirical content for each of the sustainability topics. As shown in Table 2b, the topics that organizations quantified most often were energy (38.7%) and waste (32.2%). The topics least often quantified were public engagement with sustainability (7.3%) and health, well-being, and work (5%).

RQ3 asked if there were any differences in the amount of sustainability content (number of topics) among nonprofit organizations, colleges/universities, and corporations. To answer RQ3, a one-way analysis of variance with bonferroni post hoc comparisons compared the amount of sustainability content presented by the three organization types. Results showed that the amount of sustainability content was presented significantly differently on different types of websites,

TABLE 2B
Presence of Sustainability Content (With Empirical Data) on Websites

Sustainability Topics	Total[a]	Nonprofit[b]	Company[c]	University[d]
Energy	38.7%	1.0%	55.0%	60.0%
Waste	32.3%	0.0%	47.0%	50.0%
Water	28.0%	2.0%	47.0%	35.0%
Building	26.7%	2.0%	24.0%	44.0%
Air and climate	26.0%	0.0%	41.0%	36.0%
Transportation	20.0%	0.0%	22.0%	38.0%
Dining services/food	17.7%	2.0%	8.0%	43.0%
Purchasing	15.7%	1.0%	31.0%	15.0%
Sustainability curriculum	13.0%	2.0%	4.0%	33.0%
Sustainability research	11.7%	2.0%	4.0%	29.0%
Investment	11.7%	1.0%	32.0%	2.0%
Campus engagement with sustainability	11.3%	0.0%	7.0%	27.0%
Grounds	10.7%	0.0%	9.0%	23.0%
Public engagement with sustainability	7.3%	0.0%	13.0%	9.0%
Health, well-being, and work	5.0%	0.0%	13.0%	2.0%
Diversity and affordability	1.3%	0.0%	4.0%	0.0%

Note. Websites $N = 100$.
[a]$N = 300$. [b]$n = 100$. [c]$n = 100$. [d]$n = 100$.

TABLE 3
Amount of Sustainability Content as a Difference of the Types of Website

	University Website	Company Website	Nonprofit Organization Website
M	13.66[a]	10.79[b]	.62[c]
SD	2.44	7.77	8.65

Note. Websites $N = 100$. $F(2, 297) = 100.42$, $p < .001$, partial $\eta^2 = .04$. Means with no subscript in common differ at $p < .05$ using Holm's sequential bonferroni post hoc comparisons.

$F(2, 297) = 100.42$, $p < .001$, partial $\eta^2 = .04$. Specifically, as shown in Table 3, college/university websites included the most sustainability content ($M = 13.66$, $SD = 2.44$), followed by company websites ($M = 10.79$, $SD = 7.77$) and nonprofit organizations' websites ($M = 0.62$, $SD = 8.65$).

RQ4 asked which type of organization is communicating most about sustainability initiatives that include employees and stakeholder involvement. Because fewer than five nonprofit websites communicated about most of the topics, that organization type was eliminated from the analysis conducted for this research question. To answer RQ4, a 2 × 2 chi-square analysis was performed using college/university and corporate sites. Our analysis revealed that organizations communicated differently about sustainability initiatives, $\chi^2(2, N = 200) = 16.23$,

TABLE 4A
Communicating Sustainability Initiatives from Two Types of Organization Websites

	University Website	Company Website
Either employee or stakeholder involvement information	26%$_a$	21%$_b$
Both employee and stakeholder involvement information	46%$_a$	24%$_b$

Note. Websites $N = 100$. $\chi^2(2, N = 200) = 16.23, p < .001$, Cramer's $V = .29$. Percentages with no subscript in common differ at $p < .05$ using Holm's Sequential Bonferroni post hoc comparison.

$p < .001$, Cramer's $V = .29$. Significantly, as shown in Table 4a, college/university websites communicated more about either employees or stakeholder involvement information (26%) than company websites (21%). In addition, college/university websites communicated more about both employee and stakeholder involvement information (46%) than company websites (24%).

To see what type of organization communicated most about employee involvement, a chi-square analysis was applied. Our analysis revealed that the organization types communicated differently about employee involvement, $\chi^2(1, N = 200) = 6.52$, $p < .05$, Cramer's $V = .18$. Significantly, as shown in Table 4b, college/university websites (55%) communicated more about employee involvement than company websites (37%).

To examine what type of organization communicated most about stakeholder involvement, a chi-square analysis was employed. Results revealed that organization types communicated differently about stakeholder involvement, $\chi^2(1, N = 200) = 19.27, p < .001$, Cramer's $V = .31$. Specifically, as shown in

TABLE 4B
Communicating Employee Involvement from Two Types of Organization Websites

	University Website	Company Website
Employee involvement	55%$_a$	37%$_b$

Note. Websites $N = 100$. $\chi^2(1, N = 200) = 6.52, p < .05$, Cramer's $V = .18$. Percentages with no subscript in common differ at $p < .05$ using Holm's Sequential Bonferroni post hoc comparison.

TABLE 4C
Communicating Stakeholder Involvement from Two Types of Organization Websites

	University Website	Company Website
Stakeholder involvement	63%$_a$	32%$_b$

Note. Websites $N = 100$. $\chi^2(1, N = 200) = 19.27, p < .001$, Cramer's $V = .31$. Percentages with no subscript in common differ at $p < .05$ using Holm's Sequential Bonferroni post hoc comparison.

Table 4c, college/university websites (63%) communicated more about stakeholder involvement than company websites (32%).

DISCUSSION

This study examined the websites of 300 of the top companies, nonprofits, and colleges/universities to determine what content they communicated about sustainability. Guided by the GRI and STARS frameworks, the study focused on the environmental dimensions of sustainability and compared the presence of sustainability topics and content on the sites.

One of the most telling results was the stark contrast between the number of nonprofits and the number of colleges/universities that provide sustainability content on their websites. Of the 100 nonprofits sites examined in this study, only four had a sustainability landing page on their sites, whereas nearly all (93 of 100) colleges/ universities had a landing page. This suggests that nonprofit organizations either do not have the resources or interest to communicate about the sustainability that they engage in, or have not been focusing on sustainability efforts. Either way, the findings indicate that nonprofits have much room for improvement in this area. Recent research suggests that engaging in CSR and sustainability practices has significant positive reputational benefits for nonprofits (Waters & Ott, 2015), meaning the efforts to implement and communicate about sustainability initiatives would not only reap organizational and management benefits but also improve stakeholder perception.

On the other hand, the top colleges and universities have strongly embraced sustainability as a concept, and most dedicate a portion of their website to reporting their actions. More than half of the corporations in this study had a sustainability landing page (62 of 100), which also suggests a strong commitment to communicating about sustainability. However, only 12% of the websites of any of the organization types defined the term *sustainability*. Sustainability is an evolving concept, and it has been defined many ways over the years. Organizations should be clear in their communication about what sustainability means to them and how they define it.

The sustainability communication content on the websites was primarily related to planning and reporting content, suggesting that organizations are talking about their strategic plans, programming, media communication, and formal reports. This was followed in frequency by stakeholder engagement, including employee engagement. As discussed earlier, stakeholder engagement is critical to building support for sustainability, and engagement with key stakeholders can lead to more effective decision making. The study results suggest that colleges and universities are engaging with stakeholders, including employees, more than corporations on their websites, though corporations may be engaging more with stakeholders in other ways. In many cases, colleges/universities may have more opportunity to engage with stakeholders because they are physically located in the same place as their stakeholders and can have frequent interactions; however, with a strong digital presence and other channels of communication, corporations also have an opportunity to invite stakeholders to engage in sustainability topics.

The most popular sustainability topics discussed on the websites were waste (50%), energy (48%), building (45.3%), and water (45.3%). The least popular were health, well-being, and work (17%) and diversity and affordability (10.3%). The topics that are most closely related to the environment and environmental impacts were discussed more often than socially focused consequences of environmental damage. Organizations may feel less knowledgeable and qualified to manage and report on the socially focused topics, and therefore that may be why they do not discuss the topics on their sites.

One way that organizations can build legitimacy for their sustainability programs is through communicating empirically about their impacts and efforts. In this study, organizations tended to communicate measurable, specific numbers most often for their energy use (38.7%), waste (32.3%), water use (28%), building impacts (26.7%), air and climate (26%), and transportation (20%). Measuring these impacts is fundamental to the two popular frameworks used in this study, GRI and STARS. Looking only at the college/universities and corporations, around half of the organizations in the study reported empirical data for their waste and water usage. More effort should be made by all the organization types to track and report this information as a way to demonstrate transparency and to support any claims the organizations make about improving their sustainability performance.

Limitations

This study is not without its limitations. Although a multisector examination of sustainability content on webpages offers new insight, there may be flaws in the assumption that a comparison of nonprofit organizations, colleges/universities, and corporations can exist. This study did not account for industry differences, which clearly can impact the amount of sustainability content included on web pages, specifically in the corporate and nonprofit categories. A future examination should account for key industry and interest differences when examining this topic. Furthermore, as this study used GRI and STARS guidelines as a template for measurement, it is worth noting that certain categories were derived from tools developed for specific audiences (e.g., STARS guidelines were developed specifically for higher education institutions), which impacts results. Finally, this study examined sustainability communication efforts on web pages across three sectors. This is just one mean of communication to probe this phenomenon. Future research should further explore other communication channels to fully measure stakeholder engagement efforts.

CONCLUSIONS

Overall, this study made a number of useful contributions to the literature by identifying the types of sustainability content currently being communicated on the websites of three types of organizations. Future studies should build on this study through interviews with professional communicators in these three sectors. Furthermore, the fact that only four nonprofits had a sustainability landing page on their website limited the usefulness of the findings for that organization type. More research needs to be done to understand the challenges that nonprofits face in communicating about sustainability.

By examining the types of sustainability content on organization websites, including their communication content, sustainability topics, amount of quantification, and trends among the three different types of organizations (colleges/universities, nonprofits, and corporations), this study offers a starting place for organizations that want to build their credibility in the area of sustainability. As nearly half of the organizations in this study were communicating about categories of sustainability that have the largest impact on the environment and climate—waste, energy, and water—organizations that are just beginning to develop sustainability content should start with these topics, as they are clearly viewed by the top organizations as the most relevant to sustainability. Also, these topics are more often measured and reported quantitatively. Communicators should push their organizations to match the transparency of many of the organizations in these groups that share measureable, specific impacts of their sustainability efforts. Also, approximately 30% of these top organizations are engaging with key stakeholders on sustainability-related topics on their websites. Organizations that want to build their legitimacy and create greater support for their sustainability programs should strengthen their effort to dialog with employees, customers, and other stakeholder groups.

ACKNOWLEDGMENTS

We thank the Arthur W. Page Center for Integrity in Public Communication for the sponsorship of this research.

REFERENCES

Association for the Advancement of Sustainability in Higher Education. (n.d.). The Sustainability Tracking, Assessment & Rating System. Retrieved from https://stars.aashe.org/

Baesler, E. J., & Burgoon, J. K. (1994). The temporal effects of story and statistical evidence on belief change. *Communication Research, 21*(5), 582–602. doi:10.1177/009365094021005002

Bortree, D. S. (2009). The impact of green initiatives on environmental legitimacy and Admiration of the organization. *Public Relations Review, 35*(2), 133–135. doi:10.1016/j.pubrev.2009.01.002

Bortree, D. S. (2011). The state of environmental communication: A survey of PRSA members. *Public Relations Journal, 5*(1), 1–17.

Bortree, D. S. (2014). The state of CSR communication research: A summary and future direction. *Public Relations Journal, 8*(3). Retrieved from http://www.prsa.org/Intelligence/PRJournal/Vol8/No3/

Capriotti, P., & Moreno, A. (2007). Corporate citizenship and public relations: The importance and interactivity of social responsibility issues on corporate websites. *Public Relations Review, 33*(1), 84–91. doi:10.1016/j.pubrev.2006.11.012

Craig, C. A., & Allen, M. W. (2013). Sustainability information sources: Employee knowledge, perceptions, and learning. *Journal of Communication Management, 17*(4), 292–307. doi:10.1108/JCOM-05-2012-0035

De Lange, D. E. (2013). How do universities make progress? Stakeholder-related mechanisms affecting adoption of sustainability in university curricula. *Journal of Business Ethics, 118*(1), 103–116. doi:10.1007/s10551-012-1577-y

Du, S., Bhattacharya, C. B., & Sen, S. (2010). Maximizing business returns to corporate social responsibility (CSR): The role of CSR communication. *International Journal of Management Reviews, 12*(1), 8–19. doi:10.1111/j.1468-2370.2009.00276.x

Fien, J. (2002). Advancing sustainability in higher education: Issues and opportunities for research. *Higher Education Policy, 15*, 143–152. doi:10.1016/S0952-8733(02)00005-3

Figge, C. (2011, April 22). *Sustainability: Defining the undefinable.* Retrieved from http://www.triplepundit.com/2011/04/what-is-sustainability/

Frankental, P. (2001). Corporate social responsibility–a PR invention? *Corporate Communications: An International Journal, 6*(1), 18–23. doi:10.1108/13563280110381170

Freeman, R. E. (1984). *Strategic management: A stakeholder approach.* Boston, MA: Pitman.

Global Reporting Initiative. (n.d.). *About GRI.* Retrieved from https://www.globalreporting.org/information/about-gri/Pages/default.aspx

Hall, M. R. (2006). Corporate philanthropy and corporate community relations: Measuring relationship-building results. *Journal of Public Relations Research, 18*(1), 1–21. doi:10.1207/s1532754xjprr1801_1

Hayes, A. F., & Krippendorff, K. (2007). Answering the call for a standard reliability measure for coding data. *Communication Methods and Measures, 1*(1), 77–89.

Hong, S. Y., & Rim, H. (2010). The influence of customer use of corporate websites: Corporate social responsibility, trust, and word-of-mouth communication. *Public Relations Review, 36*(4), 389–391. doi:10.1016/j.pubrev.2010.08.002

Juwaheer, T. D., Pudaruth, S., & Noyaux, M. M. E. (2012). Analysing the impact of green marketing strategies on consumer purchasing patterns in Mauritius. *World Journal of Entrepreneurship, Management and Sustainable Development, 8*(1), 36–59. doi:10.1108/20425961211221615

Ki, E.-J., & Shin, S. (2014, May). *Organization sustainability communication (OSC): Similarities and differences of OSC messages in the United States and South Korea.* Paper presented at the meeting of the International Communication Association, Seattle, WA.

Kim, S., & Ferguson, M. T. (2014). Public expectations of CSR communication: What and how to communicate CSR. *Public Relations Journal, 8*(3). Retrieved from http://www.prsa.org/Intelligence/PRJournal/Vol8/No3/

Kim, S., & Lee, Y. J. (2012). The complex attribution process of corporate social responsibility motives. *Public Relations Review, 38*, 168–170. doi:10.1016/j.pubrev.2011.09.024

Kim, S., & Rader, S. (2010). What they can do versus how much they care: Assessing corporate communication strategies on *Fortune* 500 web sites. *Journal of Communication Management, 14*(1), 59–80. doi:10.1108/13632541011017816

Klettner, A., Clarke, T., & Boersma, M. (2014). The governance of corporate sustainability: Empirical insights into the development, leadership and implementation of responsible business strategy. *Journal of Business Ethics*, *122*(1), 145–165.

KPMG. (2011). *KPMG International Survey of Corporate Responsibility Reporting 2011*. Retrieved from http://www.kpmg.com/PT/pt/.../corporate-responsibility2011.pdf.

Manetti, G., & Toccafondi, S. (2014). Defining the content of sustainability reports in nonprofit organizations: Do stakeholders really matter? *Journal of Nonprofit & Public Sector Marketing*, *26*(1), 35–61. doi:10.1080/10495142.2013.857498

Marchiori, E., Inversini, A., & Cantoni, L. (2010). *Measuring the online reputation of sustainable tourism destinations*. Presented at the 14th International Conference on Corporate Reputation, Brand, Identity, and Competitiveness, Rio de Janero, Brazil.

Mincer, J. (2008, October 6). The color of money: Sustainability has become more than a buzzword among corporations; It has become smart business. *Wall Street Journal* (Eastern ed.). Retrieved from http://online.wsj.com/article/SB122305414262702711.html

Montiel, I. (2008). Corporate social responsibility and corporate sustainability: Separate pasts, common futures. *Organization & Environment*, *21*(3), 245–269. doi:10.1177/1086026608321329

Riffe, D., Lacy, S., & Fico, F. (2013). *Analyzing media messages: Using quantitative content analysis in research* (3rd ed.). New York, NY: Routledge.

Sass, E. (2008). *Consumers consider sustainability in choosing brands*. MediaPost Publications. Retrieved online from http://publications.mediapost.com/index.cfm?fuseaction=Articles.showArticleHomePage&art aid=74117

Shriberg, M. (2002). Institutional assessment tools for sustainability in higher education: Strengths, weaknesses, and implications for practice and theory. *Higher Education Policy*, *15*(2), 153–167. doi:10.1016/S0952-8733(02)00006-5

Signitzer, B., & Prexl, A. (2008). Corporate sustainability communications: Aspects of theory and professionalization. *Journal of Public Relations Research*, *20*(1), 1–19. doi:10.1080/10627260701726996

Thomas, T. E., & Lamm, E. (2012). Legitimacy and organizational sustainability. *Journal of Business Ethics*, *110*(2), 191–203. doi:10.1007/s10551-012-1421-4

Val, M. R. R., Zinenko, A., & Montiel, I. (2011, December). Corporate social responsibility instruments and the new ISO 26000. *In Proceedings of the International Association for Business and Society*, *22*, 316–326.

Van Marrewijk, M. (2003). Concepts and definitions of CSR and corporate sustainability: Between agency and communion. *Journal of Business Ethics*, *44*(2–3), 95–105. doi:10.1023/A:1023331212247

Waters, R. D., & Ott, H. K. (2015, March). *Testing for-profit and non-profit organizations' corporate social responsibility messaging with the public: Credibility, believability and formality*. Paper presented at the meeting of the International Public Relations Research Conference, Miami, FL.

World Commission on Environment and Development. (1987). *Our common future* (Report). Retrieved from the United Nations General Assembly website: http://www.un-documents.net/our-common-future.pdf

Zoch, L. M., Collins, E. L., & Sisco, H. F. (2008). From communication to action: The use of core framing tasks in public relations messages on activist organizations' web sites. *Public Relations Journal*, *2*(4), 1–23.

Index

INDEX

digitally mediated political activism 64–5; in China *see* anti-PX protests, traditional and digital media; cycles of contention 66–7; diffusion of contention 67–8; "modular repertoires" 66–7; recurrent mechanism of 64, 68, 80; repertoire of contention 66

Energy Nation campaign 51
Energy Tomorrow campaign 52, 59
environmental marketplace advocacy campaigns 46
Environmental Protection Agency (EPA) 44, 53–4

Farm Talk radio program *see* Community Markets for Conservation's *Farm Talk* (COMACO's *Farm Talk*)
fossil fuel industries, U.S.: America's everyman/everywoman 51–2; circuit of culture model *see* circuit of culture model; and electric utility industry 45; marketplace advocacy 45–6; "moral majority," industry supporters as 56, 57; overview of 43–5, 56–8; paternal caretaker for citizens 55–6; president's action plan 44; study limitations 59
framing 11–14

Gaither, Barbara Miller 2
Gaither, T. Kenn 2
Global Reporting Initiative (GRI) 133, 135, 141
global warming 44
GRI *see* Global Reporting Initiative

Hall, Stuart 46, 48, 50
Hmielowski, Jay D. 3

institutional trust 31, **33**, 34

Jere, Filius 88
Johnson, Richard 46
Jun Liu 2–3

Kim, Sei-Hill 2
Krippendorff's alpha 136

Lewis, Dale 87
Lindenfeld, Laura 2

Ma, Dong Hoon 2
marketplace advocacy 45–6, 59, 60
Mass Communication and Society 1
mass communication research, in sustainability science: agenda-setting process 14–16; framing 11–14; overview of 7–8; role of 7, 14; social-ecological systems 9; stakeholder-inclusive approach 9; traditional transmission model 10; in transdisciplinary context 17–18; "wicked problems" 8
mass self-mobilization 76–7
McComas, Katherine 3
meaning creation process 48
media's role in sustainable agriculture *see* Community Markets for Conservation's *Farm Talk* (COMACO's *Farm Talk*)
moderated multiple regression method 34
"modular repertoires" 66–7

Nisbet, Erik C. 3

organization sustainability communication (OSC) 131–2
organization websites, sustainability communication on: coding scheme 134–6; descriptive analysis 136–7; features on **137**; intercoder reliability test and coding 136; limitations 142; message content 132; overview of 130–1; reporting standards 133; research design 134; sampling procedure 134; stakeholder theory 133–4; sustainable topics **138**, **139**, 142; types of **140**
OSC *see* organization sustainability communication
Ott, Holly 3

participatory-based research methods 19
political activism, digital media and *see* digitally mediated political activism
"process of translation" 48

repertoire of contention, digital media as 66, 79–80

science media use 29–32; and mobile technology 40; responsibility attribution and 35
SES *see* social-ecological systems

INDEX